TAROT & THE UNCONSCIOUS

A Freudian Perspective

BRYAN DE JUSTIN

© 2025 Bryan de Justin. All rights reserved.

ISBN: 979-8-9987581-6-4

No part of this book may be reproduced, stored in a retrieval system, or transmitted in any form or by any means—electronic, mechanical, photocopying, recording, or otherwise—without prior written permission from the author or publisher, except as permitted by U.S. copyright law.

This publication is intended to provide accurate and authoritative information regarding the subject matter covered. It is sold with the understanding that neither the author nor the publisher is engaged in rendering legal, financial, accounting, medical, mental-health, pharmaceutical, or other professional services. The material is provided "as is," without warranties of any kind, express or implied, including but not limited to implied warranties of merchantability or fitness for a particular purpose. No warranty may be created or extended by sales representatives or written sales materials. The advice and strategies contained herein may not be suitable for your situation; you should consult a qualified professional when appropriate. Neither the author nor the publisher shall be liable for any commercial or personal damages, including but not limited to special, incidental, consequential, or other damages.

Written by Bryan de Justin

Trademarks: Product names and brands mentioned herein are the property of their respective owners.

Printed in the United States of America.

*To **Leticia Jimenez-Trujillo**,*

My mother, who has all due honour and respect as the prime element of my person and this book. My first written work, and all the rest, are yours.
To you, who are the fount of all my creativity, love, and life. May this book exist forever as an emblem of my love for you.

"The Tarot embodies symbolical presentations of universal ideas, behind which lie all the implicits of the human mind, and it is in this sense that they contain secret doctrine, which is the realization by the few of truths imbedded in the consciousness of all, though they have not passed into express recognition by ordinary people."
- Arthur Edward Waite

PREFACE

The history of Psychology, Mysticism, and the Occult are so deeply embedded that it can be said that the pillars of Psychology are both Mysticism and the Occult. What separates these two pillars is that, within the former, we have a philosophical perspective of life and existence with no experimentation; and in the latter, we have experimentation with no philosophy of life and existence. Psychology, however, achieves what Mysticism and Occultism cannot – it is both experimental and philosophical. Though Freud referred to the Occult as 'the black tide of mud' (Jung, 1963), he could not reject the psychic dimension of psychology, remaining open to conceptualisations of telepathy and other psychic phenomena (Freud, 1922/1955; 1935).

Modern psychology, especially American, lacks focus on the soul. I do not refer to 'the soul' here as a spiritual essence – though it may be applied to those who believe in it. Rather, I refer to the soul as the emotional, personological, and mental aspect of the individual. American psychology is heavily entrenched in the neuropsychiatric model. Though I am not an opponent of medicine or psychiatry, I am indeed opposed to reducing the passions, jealousies, betrayals, sorrows, and euphorias of individuals down to numbers. Because of this, what we now have in the field of modern psychology is a dilution of the soul.

Modern society has ceased to see itself as the centre of the universe and man as a reflection of a greater universal whole. Now, we are simply a point on the great universal map – this universal map being yet another point amid an ocean of many other universes. Though modern science has heralded the greatest inventions in history, it has also heralded the view that we are fleeting, transitory, and merely a number. After the 'Enlightenment', forests ceased to indwell dancing nymphs, ponds no longer have spirits, and caves no longer have demons.

Modern science convinces society that dreams, imaginations, and fantasies do not exist. If one were truly to heed such Mephistophelian advice, we would be neglecting a profound aspect of our essence, ultimately convincing ourselves that we, in fact, do not exist. Unfortunately, this frame of mind is prevalent, even on cultural levels, leading to the dismissal of emotions and a sentimental frigidity. Awareness of our internal world leads to personal edification; lack of self-awareness, however, leads to self-destruction. It is precisely the attainment of self-illumination that psychoanalysis values so ardently as its golden law. No psychoanalysis can be successful without it. In fact, psychoanalysis and self-awareness are inseparable. Nothing can be considered psychoanalysis without the presence of *anagnorisis*.

I shall discuss this principle of self-illumination shortly; however, I shall not fail to mention here that it is a cardinal element of the purpose of this book.

The content regarding Jungian or analytical interpretations of the Tarot abounds as plentifully as water within the sea. However, the Freudian or psychoanalytic interpretations are scarce. The few places that mention them either do so only referentially or offer little interpretation; rather, they express criticism in some regards (Wang & Wang, 2008). The only person I have encountered who has taken a considerate approach to this subject, though briefly, is Rosengarten (2000).

Thus, I present this, my first written work – composed over the span of a year – as a psychoanalytic interpretation of the Tarot. Given that there are so many expositions of Jungian and analytical interpretations of the Tarot (see Nichols, 1980), I have resolved to remain psychoanalytic. Yet, though I remain as psychoanalytical as possible, I have found it impossible to neglect offering circumstantial attention to Jung and depth psychology.

This book is not primarily for the occultist, though I do not disbelieve that it may serve him in some capacity. Rather, this book is intended for the psychological, parapsychological, and academic researcher, though it would indeed be difficult for the occultist not to be considered a researcher.

The ideas in this book were developed and written over the course of 2024 and 2025. It is my hope that it serves as a catalyst for future researchers and other psychoanalytically inclined individuals to explore the Tarot. In doing so, I hope that the burgeoning field of Tarot psychology and psychotherapy will continue to flourish.

To the critic, I can only offer this book as explanation. If this does not suffice, all I have left to say is: experience it for yourself. Then, and only then, shall you understand.

Lastly, to the psychoanalyst who fears leaving the domain of science: *remember that Science, Mythology, Philosophy, and Mysticism are one. For in all, man seeks to know himself.*

INTRODUCTION

Carl Jung is almost immutably accredited with establishing the relationship between Tarot and psychology explicitly. However, this is not precisely the case.

The relationship between Tarot and psychology developed dynamically in the early part of the twentieth century. Paul Foster Case, a member of the occult society *The Hermetic Order of the Golden Dawn*, made this relationship explicitly clear in his work *The Tarot: A Key to the Wisdom of the Ages* (1920). In it, he states that "The Tarot is a key to the wisdom of the ages, and it can reveal the secrets of *human personality [emphasis added]* and the laws of *personal development [emphasis added]*." Expounding on the Tarot as a tool for self-realisation and the integration of consciousness and unconsciousness (*anagnorisis*), he explains: "Each card in the Tarot deck represents an *archetypal image [emphasis added]* that speaks to the universal experiences and stages of human development. By studying these images, we can gain a deeper understanding of our own psychological and spiritual journey."

Fascinatingly, not only does Case establish the Tarot as

a reflection of the internal world and a tool for psychological growth, he also definitively identifies the cards as psychological archetypes – almost a decade prior to Jung's first direct integration (1927), and fourteen years before his solidified work on archetypal psychology (1934).

Case's initiatory studies in psychology prepared the way for his occult research. In 1901, he met the occultist Claude Fayette Bragdon, who, during a game of playing cards, asked: "Case, where do you suppose playing cards came from?" (Case, 2006) This small question, containing a broad and profound answer, catalysed Case's lifelong study of the Tarot.

Case's first publication regarding the Tarot appeared in 1916 in *The Word*, a journal dedicated to philosophy and theosophical studies. In it, he draws connections between pictorial symbols and the Hebrew alphabet by tracing their archaic derivatives and their historical progression into their modern forms. For instance, he begins his article by introducing the Hebrew letter *Daleth*, noting that its original form was that of a triangle.

This pictorial letter survived in Greek, recognised as 'Delta'. Later, it was Latinised into the Roman alphabet as the lowercase letter 'd' that we use today (Case, 1916). He details that the Greeks derived their alphabet from the Phoenicians and identifies Delta as a feminine letter. He explains that the ancient form of Delta had the apex pointing downward, a yonic symbol of femininity and a mystical symbol of the element of water. In phallicism, the triangle with the apex pointing upwards is phallic and represents the masculine principle and the element of fire (Chevalier & Gheerbrant, 1996). Thus, he concludes: "Daleth represents the womb."

Child psychoanalyst Melanie Klein likewise opined that children project their internal world onto the alphabet, channelling their emotions through reading and writing. She corroborates this by noting that the Latin alphabet, like that of the Chinese, is pictorial (1923). To Klein, this explained scholastic difficulties, as the activities of reading and writing served as channels for the discharge of libido; as a result, the instincts or internal world are expressed through the libidinal cathexis itself. In her case with little Fritz, she demonstrates how the letter 'I' was symbolic of the penis and the 'O' of the vagina. She likewise refers to Abraham (1923), who pointed out the symbolic meaning of the number '3', derived from the Oedipal situation (mother, father, child) as well as from the male genitals.

Allen Dundes, a psychoanalytic folklorist, also wrote on the presence and importance of the number three (Dundes, 1979). Among many examples, he notes that in numerous jokes (which are the equivalents of fairy tales), there are three principles, for instance, a blonde, a brunette, and a redhead; or "three people walk into a bar", and so forth.

There are three persons that compose the all-male Holy Trinity: God the Father, God the Son, and God the Holy Spirit. There are also three times of day (morning, evening, night); the phrase "three times a charm"; riddles are often in a triadic form, as in the riddle of the Sphinx; three stages of man (child, adult, elder); Tic-Tac-Toe is played with three rows of three; in sports, "three strikes and you're out"; Americans often eat three meals a day. In Kabbalah, people are divided into three parts: Nefesh, Ruach, and Neshama. In elementary school, children are taught the phrase "Reading, 'Riting, and 'Rithmetic". Lower education consists of three levels: elementary, secondary, and preparatory; upper education consists of three levels as well: bachelor's, master's, and doctorate. The world is divided into three: liquid, solid, and gaseous. In physical anthropology, the races of men are divided into three: Caucasoid,

INTRODUCTION

Mongoloid, and Negroid. The European race is divided into three: Nordic, Alpine, and Mediterranean. The branches of American government are divided into three: executive, judicial, and legislative.

There are three political institutions that possess executive and judicial authority in the European Union: the Council, the Parliament, and the Commission. The Oedipus complex is characterised by three actors: mother, father, and child. These, among many other instances, are demonstrative. In the Tarot, three is also a prevalent number: three women in the Three of Cups, three architects in the Three of Pentacles, three figures in the Seven of Swords, three figures in The Lovers and The Devil, and three pyramids in the Page of Wands. The Hierophant has three figures, the papal cross with three horizontal lines, the papal tiara with three tiers (triregnum), and three crosses on the papal robes.

Dundes states that the precise origin and explanation for the significance of the number three are difficult to ascertain definitively, but he provides multiple explanations, all of which, the writer opines, are accurate. Firstly, the religious symbolism of the Godhead, bearing so much psychological weight on man, is reflected in his organisation of the external world. The family is also divided into three (father, mother, and child), explaining cultural symbolisations that manifest in the external world as well. Regardless of the explanation, Dundes affirms that the relationship between man and the number three is both significant and symbolic, representing essential aspects of human life.

Case, in his 1916 publication, affirms (incredibly) the importance of the number three as well, stating that the most important designs of the Major Arcana are those that are multiples of three. These are The Empress (3), The

Lovers (6), The Hermit (9), The Hanged Man (12), The Devil (15), The Moon (18), and The World (21). These represent the stages of the Magician's progression in his internal journey. The Empress represents the amplification of the Magician's inchoate mental energy. It is afterwards channelised with the Magician's mate, also representative of the internal masculine and feminine principles aimed towards transcendental themes (*The Lovers*). *The Hermit* represents the attainment of inner illumination, followed by its subsequent price, demonstrated by *The Hanged Man*. *The Devil* is the symbol of primitivism, the unacceptable, and taboo, which must be dissolved. *The Moon* represents the sublimation of this internal darkness, followed by completion and purpose in *The World*.

We can approach this schema alternatively, psychoanalytically, when we consider it as a representation of ego development. *The Empress* represents the home life of the child, followed by his release outward into the world and the exploration of mature relationships in *The Lovers*. This is followed by the attainment of maturity (*The Hermit*) and the subsequent necessity of ego transformation (*The Hanged Man*). *The Devil* represents the Id and the repressed contents of the psyche that one must confront lest one be controlled by the Id and unconscious impulses. *The Moon* represents the sublimation of these feelings, and *The World* is the culmination of the ego's development and the sense of completeness that results.

Case clearly pointed out Dundes' important aspects of life (that is, critical stages and aspects of ego development) reflected in the number three, as the individual (*The Magician*) progresses from nurturing and dependency (*The Empress*) to the resolution of internal conflicts (*The Lovers*), introspection (*The Hermit*), transformation (*The Hanged Man*), confrontation with the Id (*The Devil*), sublimation of the unconscious (*The Moon*), and the achievement of wholeness (*The World*). It appears Case understood very well the dynamics of projection and identification, and their relationship with the arcanum and symbols.

Jeff Burr, Cht., in his seminar on the applications of Tarot in personal psychology (2016), explicitly divides the Major Arcana into three. The first seven cards symbolise forces of the outside world that influence the individual. Eight through fourteen are internal reflections of aspects of ourselves. Fifteen through twenty-one represent universal and all-encompassing influences upon our lives.

It must also be expressly noted that Case's *The Tarot* preceded Jung's fundamental expositions on archetypes (1921; 1927; 1934–1954; 1938). However, the concept of symbols, myth, and their presence in the internal world of individuals, as well as within cultures and religions, had already been conceived, most notably by Freud (1900; 1910; 1913). Freud established the groundwork for symbolism and myth in psychology. Case studied psychology prior to his involvement in the occult, so these psychological ideas likely nourished his later occult ones, thereby enabling him to identify the connection between occult symbols and personal psychology.

Prior to Case's syncretic 1920 work on the Tarot and Jung's *Symbols of Transformation* (1912), Freud explored symbols and myth extensively and regarded them as essential components of psychoanalysis. In his foundational work *The Interpretation of Dreams* (1900), he concretises the myth of *Oedipus Rex* as the psychological foundation of neurosis and psychosexual development. He stated that the reason why the myth of *Oedipus Rex* moves us so profoundly, to the point where it has been preserved through the centuries, is because his destiny could have been our own during infancy. Likewise, he utilised the myth of Saturn castrating his father Uranus as the symbolic representation of oedipal competition and castration anxiety.

Regarding this castration anxiety, he affirmed that it reaches into the great mythological representations of nations, and it colours their religious creations, as well as the dreams of individual beings. (Freud, 1909/1955) The hero who overcomes the monster in the dragon fight—what more is he than a representative of the ego, which, in its emergence from the primary stage of infancy, overcomes the dangers of the world of instinct and emerges as a unique entity? (Neumann, 1954/2014)

He also describes the victory of Jupiter over his father Saturn, who at first devoured him, as representative of the return of the repressed, whereby what is repressed into unconsciousness returns in darker and more confrontational forms (Freud 1900/2010). He parallels the process of dream interpretation and the enigma of the unconscious mind with the riddle of the Sphinx. He also recognises the myth of Orestes avenging his father's death by killing his mother as illustrative of the progressed Oedipus complex, as well as the presence of vengeance, guilt, and love in family relations.

In *The Origins and Development of Psychoanalysis* (1910), Freud, in addition to the previously discussed myths and symbols, discussed the symbol of the "primal horde", a mythological and anthropological motif wherein a primal horde, led by a dominant male, is overthrown by a younger male who then establishes rules and norms to regulate their society. He also introduced the impact of totemism and taboo upon culture, society, and morals as regulators of the unconscious mind and primitive impulses. This would later be greatly expanded in his 1913 work *Totem and Taboo*.

In 1920, Freud published *Beyond the Pleasure Principle*,

INTRODUCTION

where he famously introduced the life and death instincts. He named these two instincts Eros (the Roman deity Cupid), god of passionate love, and Thanatos, the god of death. Eros represents the set of life instincts that drive individuals towards survival, reproduction, love, and pleasure. These instincts are associated with growth, development, and the creation of life. Thanatos, on the other hand, embodies the death instincts. These are the unconscious drives that push individuals towards aggression, self-destruction, and a return to an inorganic state (death). Freud proposed this concept to explain masochistic and self-sabotaging behaviours that seem to go against the pleasure principle. He named the two fundamental instincts of the human being after these symbolic and mythological deities.

A notable mention as well is Otto Rank, one of Freud's close associates, who wrote *The Myth and Birth of the Hero* (1909). Psychoanalytic ideas of mythology are greatly illustrated in this work. Rank expounds on common patterns across heroic myths: miraculous births, early dangers, divine intervention, and eventual triumph. Rank saw this as representative of psychological processes. The miraculous birth represents the child's narcissism and his unique position in the world. Early endangerment shortly after birth (for instance, Satan seeking the destruction of the child Jesus through Herod, or the child Hercules, who was sent two serpents by Hera to envenom him) represents the infant's early experiences of vulnerability and dependence on caregivers, which can also reflect the child's unconscious fears of abandonment or harm. The challenges and divine interventions represent the child's developmental journey, and the eventual triumph represents the resolution of inner conflicts and the achievement of a more mature self.

He establishes that the hero's struggle against the

father symbol, such as in the case of David and Goliath, is a symbolic enactment of the child's unconscious wish to overcome paternal authority and assert his own identity. He explains that the monsters the hero overcomes (recall the seven trials of Hercules, Perseus rescuing Andromeda, St George and the Dragon, Jesus as a child subduing a dragon in a cave, Psyche lulling Cerberus with cakes, or Prince Philip battling Maleficent) are personifications of the internal anxieties and conflicts that one must overcome for psychological growth.

None of this is to say that Jung neglected the importance of symbolism. In *Symbols of Transformation* (1912), Jung established the groundwork for what would later become his archetypal psychology. In it, he described myth as portraying the transformation of the libido (psychic energy) across different processes and experiences. He stated that myth allows people to connect with their deeper selves and enables us to address psychological questions. It was only later that the value of the Tarot materialised in Jung's work, emerging first referentially in his 1928–1930 seminar given at the Psychological Club in Zürich, Switzerland. In it, he stated that the Tarot cards are really images of archetypes. Therefore, he posited, one could read a sort of psychological meaning into the Tarot cards. He exemplified how the cards of the Major Arcana (the Empress, the Fool, the Lovers, etc.) are more or less typical representations of the different stages of the individuation process. (Jung, 1933/1997)

Jung did not fail to see how these mythological and symbolic images were psychologically significant. In one instance, he noted: "One can see how these images illustrate the different stages of life, as well as the transitions and transformations one undergoes."

Psychotherapeutically, Rank saw myths as a symbolic

framework for understanding personal experience. Freud suggested that myths, like dreams, are expressions of repressed wishes and fears. Thus, by understanding these symbolic narratives, both at a cultural and individual level, psychological issues in therapy could be uncovered. Jung viewed them as translations of unconscious material into conscious expression and therefore as tools for self-discovery.

The Rider–Waite–Smith Tarot deck had been published nineteen years prior to Jung's seminars. During those nineteen years, however, the Rider–Waite–Smith deck flourished in popularity almost immediately, particularly following Waite's failure to secure its copyright in the United States (Jensen, 2005). Consequently, the renown of the Tarot spread far and wide, a fact reflected in modern times by its circulation of over one hundred million copies across twenty countries.

Freud and his contemporaries were undoubtedly familiar with it, especially considering that Freud was said to have loved playing *Tarocchi* (Jones, 1953). Although he did not write about its psychological implications, his fondness for engaging with symbolic systems in his leisure time suggests that he might have appreciated the profound symbolic meanings inherent in the Tarot. Jung even mentioned that when one plays with the Tarot cards, the unconscious plays with its contents and engages with them. One thereby enacts a kind of psychic interexchange with the cards.

This parallels Klein's 1923 work *Early Analysis*, in which she noted that children's play reflected internal dynamics and object relations. Anna Freud, in *Normality and Pathology in Childhood* (1966), illustrated this in detail through the example of boys' positions on the football field and how these reflect their social relationships with other boys as well as their own self-perception. Klein, in the same article, similarly viewed sport play as an opportunity to analyse active and passive determinants, as well as homosexual and heterosexual inclinations.

Modern psychotherapy employs these same principles of projective play therapy, as seen in sandbox therapy (Lowenfield, 1950) and video game psychotherapy (Rice, 2022). Indeed, Rosengarten (2000) also compared the utilisation of Tarot in psychotherapy with the use of free association in psychoanalysis and sandtray methods in play therapy.

Thus, regarding Tarot and psychology, Paul Foster Case and Carl Jung developed their ideas almost in parallel but within different intellectual and cultural contexts. Case's work was rooted in esoteric and occult traditions, focusing on the Tarot as a tool for spiritual insight and personal growth. Jung, on the other hand, approached symbols and archetypes from a psychological and analytical perspective, incorporating a wide range of influences, including mythology, religion, alchemy, and other occult traditions. Jung was aware of occult teachings, and, having exposited his archetypal psychology later in the century, incorporated them as well as expanded upon these ideas in his own work (Jung 1955/1963). His extensive study of symbols and mythology, combined with his interest in esoteric traditions, suggests a broad intellectual curiosity that could have intersected with the teachings of figures like Case.

Nonetheless, the intellectual material required to draw such conclusions was available prior to both Jung's and Case's publications. Case made the relationship between Tarot and psychology explicit in 1920, but the broader connection between the internal world and symbols or archetypes had already been developing through the work of Freud and his contemporaries, including Jung. Jung, influenced by or aware of occult teachings, integrated and expanded these ideas within his analytical psychology framework. Both Case and Jung contributed to the understanding of symbols and archetypes, starting from the same foundation in psychology but with distinct emphases.

As if perceiving the future of psychology, Case advised the critic that "The Tarot is not merely a tool for divination, but a guide for inner transformation. Each card holds the potential to unlock new levels of awareness and to catalyse profound changes in the seeker's inner world" (1920). In *The Tarot*, he states that it is not very profitable for the student of the Tarot to regard it as a tool for divination before regarding it as a tool for personal reflection. Case understood the projective quality of the Tarot and its ability to reflect the internal world of the viewer.

In *Moses and Monotheism* (1939), Freud delves into the profound impact of symbols on cultures and religions, exploring the origins of monotheism through the figure of Moses and the development of Jewish religious thought. Freud presents how religious symbols and myths influence individual, cultural, and collective identities.

Freud proposes that Moses was an Egyptian who introduced monotheism to the Hebrews, linking this historical narrative to the broader development of religious symbolism. He interprets the psychological underpinnings of religious beliefs and practices, as well as the Moses saga, exploring how repressed collective memories and traumas influence the formation of religious myths and symbols. While Freud does not use the term "collective unconscious", he examines the idea of a collective cultural memory, arguing that cultural and religious symbols arise from shared unconscious processes that shape collective behaviour and beliefs, as well as universal psychological experiences.

Most especially, Freud discusses how repressed events and memories can resurface in symbolic forms, influencing religious narratives and practices. On symbolism and repression, he notes, "The fate of the repressed material is that it strives to reassert itself in the form of a return of the repressed, and this reassertion often occurs in symbolic form." Here, he posits that the contents of the unconscious strive for expression (otherwise there would be no conflict), but since they are repressed, they find expression through symbolic material. This symbolic material is therefore the doorway into the repository of the unconscious, with this premise of access to the unconscious through symbols forming the cardinal principle of his dream psychology in *The Interpretation of Dreams*.

Although Freud does not explicitly use the term "archetypes", his discussion of central religious figures such as Moses can be seen as an exploration of archetypal symbols that hold profound psychological significance for cultural, individual, and religious identity. Regarding Moses as an archetypal figure, Freud states, "Moses, as a powerful leader and lawgiver, embodies the archetypal image of the father figure, whose authority and influence persist through cultural and religious traditions." He examines how religious symbols and myths shape collective identities, providing a sense of continuity and meaning for communities, and explores the psychological mechanisms through which these symbols reinforce social cohesion and cultural heritage. On collective memory, he observes, "The collective memory of a people preserves the traces of significant historical events and figures, which are often transformed into symbolic myths that shape the collective identity and cultural values of the community."

'Moses and Monotheism' does not directly discuss the Tarot, as its primary focus is on the origins and develop-

ment of monotheistic religion, specifically Judaism, and the psychological underpinnings of religious beliefs. However, we can draw some parallels and insights from Freud's exploration of symbols and their impact on culture and religion that can illuminate the Tarot in a few key ways.

Freud's discussion of religious symbols as expressions of repressed material and collective memory can be applied to the Tarot, which is rich in universal symbols and archetypal figures. Just as religious symbols carry deep psychological significance, so too do the images on Tarot cards, which represent various aspects of the human experience and psyche through mythological and symbolic designs. The Tarot contains archetypal figures such as *The Fool, the Magician*, and *The High Priestess*. Likewise, it features mythological, religious, and symbolic figures such as Adam and Eve, the Sphinx, Isis, the Virgin Mary, and others. These figures can be seen as similar to the archetypal characters Freud analyses in religious myths, such as Moses, representing universal themes and patterns that resonate with the unconscious mind.

In 1922, Freud wrote *'Medusa's Head'*, connecting the symbolism and eventual decapitation of Medusa's head with the concept of castration, arguing that the fear of Medusa represented the fear associated with the castration complex. Much later, in 1948, Gaston Bachelard coined the term *'Medusa Complex'* to describe the freezing, paralysis, and suspension of emotion. It is a form of fear rooted in the threatening parental gaze.

Freud's exploration of how cultural and religious symbols shape collective identity can be extended to the Tarot, which has evolved as a cultural artefact with deep symbolic meanings. From the beginning of their history, different countries and societies have projected their values, their surroundings, and themselves onto the cards.

For instance, the Spanish decks reflected a consciousness of royalty, heraldry, and monarchy, while the German deck reflected the life and dynamics of the countryside. The images on Tarot cards can both reflect and influence the personal and social consciousness of those who use them. It is for this reason that connections between *The Tower* (also called *The Tower of Destruction* and *The Tower of Babel*) and the 9/11 Twin Tower tragedy have been made (Adair, 2019).

The Tarot can be viewed as a symbolic narrative that parallels the way religious myths create a sense of identity and meaning for individuals and communities. Each card tells part of a story that reflects the journey of both the individual and the collective psyche.

In the same way that the mythological stories of Oedipus, Hercules, Jupiter, and others were preserved and propagated popularly because of their resonance with the internal world of humankind, so too have the Tarot cards been preserved and propagated due to their resonance with the inner world. This would also explain their explosive popularity upon publication.

The same literary and artistic propagation found in fairy tales and myth is evident in *The Green Sheaf* by Pamela Colman Smith, the illustrator of the Rider–Waite–Smith deck. *The Green Sheaf* was a magazine that ran from 1903 to 1904. It was a collective work that published art, poetry, and literature by occultists, and there are numerous references to the Tarot throughout its pages. In 2023, *The Green Sheaf* was restored and is now active once again. In 2025, I published *Testaments from Another Life*, a collection of tragic-romantic fairy tales inspired by *The Green Sheaf* and Tarot imagery.

Additionally, in 1973, Italo Calvino published *'The Castle of Crossed Destinies'*, a story about a gathering of travellers who, after passing through a mysterious forest, find themselves unable to speak. They share their stories through Tarot cards, which the narrator then interprets. To Freud, myths are retold because they symbolise fundamental human desires and conflicts that form part of our collective psychological experience, making them perpetually relevant and compelling.

The horror film *'Tarot'* (2024) tells the story of a group of teenagers who discover a cursed Tarot deck, within which the archetypes come to life in monstrous form, forcing them to confront their inner fears.

You will not find unadulterated psychology in a laboratory, a pharmacy, or a statistical chart. You will find it in a museum, in a Shakespearean play, and in ancient poetry. Dundes (1969) emphasised the sociocultural and psychological function of mythological and folkloric retelling and propagation: "Folklore is a mirror of culture, a reflection of societal values, norms, and structures. The retelling of folktales and myths ensures the transmission of these cultural elements from one generation to the next, thus maintaining cultural continuity."

This explains why older Disney films, almost a hundred years after their creation, are being retold as live-action adaptations. The Tarot, being a vessel of mythology, contains within itself a mirror of culture, societal values, norms, repressed human desires, motifs, and thematic life lessons. Hence, the premise of folkloric and mythological retelling, transmission, and propagation applies to it.

Freud's ideas about projection and the return of the repressed can thus be applied to the Tarot. The images on the cards often evoke personal and unconscious material, allowing individuals to project their inner states onto the cards and gain insight into their psyche. Similar to religious rituals that provide structure and meaning, the Tarot involves rituals such as shuffling and drawing cards, often in a structured and distinctive manner, which create an organised space for reflection and exploration of the unconscious mind.

The Tarot thus becomes a personal narrative that one constructs, perhaps most perfectly exemplified in Calvino's *'The Castle of Crossed Destinies'*. In this novel, the characters use Tarot spreads to communicate their personal stories of romance, tragedy, and drama, a process akin to the art of 'self-making' described by Jerome Bruner (1990; 1991).

Bruner, a cognitive psychologist, in his book *"Acts of Meaning"*, discusses how individuals construct their reality and self-concept through narratives. Bruner states: "Self-making is a narrative art, and the stories we tell about our lives are our attempts to create order and meaning out of the events that befall us." He emphasises the role of narratives in organising human experience and constructing personal identity, highlighting that the act of storytelling is central to how we understand ourselves and our place in the world.

Personality psychologist Dan P. McAdams (1993; 2001) also explored how personal narratives, or 'life stories', are integral to the development of identity. In his work *'The Stories We Live By'*, he writes: "Life stories are the large, integrative narratives that people construct to make sense of their lives, to provide their lives with some semblance of unity and purpose." McAdams argues that the personal narratives individuals construct are crucial for understanding how they perceive their own lives, make decisions, and find meaning and coherence in their experiences.

Psychotherapeutically, these stories can be either conducive or detrimental to the person. The role of the psychotherapist would be to work through negatively impactful stories and transform them into enriching, fortifying ones. Because stories contain unconscious material, these narratives can also be unconsciously perpetuated. Freud discussed this in *'Beyond the Pleasure Principle'* (1920), wherein he examines repetition compulsion and explores why, in some instances, an individual's friends always betray them, or why an individual's romantic involvements always end in the same way. Freud suggests that repetition compulsion is driven by unconscious processes and serves several psychological functions. It is an attempt by the psyche to gain mastery over a traumatic event or unresolved conflict. By repeatedly experiencing the trauma, the individual unconsciously seeks to work through it and achieve a different outcome, though often unsuccessfully.

He explains that this is the reason for traumatic dreams, describing them as a safe re-enactment of the traumatic event in order to master it. He adds: "The patient does not remember anything of what he has forgotten and repressed, but acts it out. He reproduces it not as a memory but as an action; he repeats it, without, of course, knowing that he is repeating it." Freud does not neglect this consideration as to why some people repeat painful experiences. He thus connects repetition compulsion to the death drive (also known as Thanatos) by suggesting that the compulsion to repeat is a manifestation of Thanatos.

Thanatos embodies an unconscious wish to return to a state of non-existence, a primary state of rest or equilibrium, akin to the inorganic state before life. While repetition compulsion can be seen as an attempt to gain mastery over past traumas, Freud suggests that it also serves a deeper, more fundamental drive towards self-destruction (masochism) and a return to an inanimate state. This is the influence of Thanatos, driving the individual to repeat distressing experiences as a way to fulfil the unconscious desire for the cessation of life and a return to an inert state. The death drive represents a movement towards the ultimate reduction of tension and a return to a state of equilibrium.

Repetition compulsion, by forcing the individual to relive traumatic experiences, aligns with this drive by attempting to bring about a resolution that returns the psyche to a state of rest. This self-defeating behaviour, encompassing not only sexual masochism but also a broader pattern of self-destructive actions, highlights the pervasive influence of Thanatos in shaping human behaviour, particularly in the realm of self-making.

The psychoanalyst must therefore analyse the personal narratives that analysands create for themselves in order to establish less negative narratives and more positive ones. Positive repetition manifests in two primary forms: practice and mastery, and routine and stability. Repeating an action to improve a skill or achieve mastery is driven by Eros, the life drive. This form of repetition aligns with the pleasure principle, as it ultimately leads to positive outcomes and personal growth. Establishing routines provides stability and predictability, which can be comforting and beneficial for mental health. This type of repetition assists in managing daily life and is not inherently connected to Thanatos.

In contrast, negative repetition involves unconsciously repeating behaviours or situations that recreate past traumas or painful experiences. Actions that lead to self-defeat, whether in relationships, careers, or personal life, reflect the influence of the death drive. These behaviours undermine the individual's well-being and are often beyond conscious control.

Pollock (1970), in his article *'Anniversary Reactions, Trauma, and Mourning'*, discusses the adverse unconscious enactment of personal mythologies. He describes a specific type of enactment called *'Anniversary Reactions'*, which refers to symptoms that occur on, but are not limited to, birthdays, death days, holidays, or any other fixed dates. These anniversaries act as triggers for the release of unconscious content.

He refers to Hilgard (1953), who gave the case of a mother who developed pneumonia, pleurisy, and psychosis when her daughter was six. It was later discovered that her father had died of pneumonia, pleurisy, and meningitis when the patient was six. She was subsequently separated from her mother as well. Hilgard explains that these clinical findings represent the eruption of the repressed, as mentioned previously, yet in ways that are often far more catastrophic than the original situation. These anniversary responses result from an identification with, and reaction to, a temporal trigger that allows the repressed conflict to emerge.

Pollock also cites hospital statistics demonstrating that large hospital samples revealed a temporal correlation between childhood loss at birth and first hospitalisation as an adult. Solidifying these as clinical phenomena, Pollock draws on several further examples. He mentions the occurrence of surviving siblings or twins identifying with their deceased sibling, believing that they too will die in a similar fashion.

He also refers to *'The Nemesis Phenomenon'*, an identificatory mechanism in which an individual believes he is destined to repeat in his own life the pattern of a significant other's life that ended in tragedy and catastrophe. In this phenomenon, there is extensive life-pattern mirroring, even in the correlation of events and ages at which certain occurrences happen. These may persist for many years, or even throughout an entire lifetime, and serve as the foundation of a detrimental personal mythology, with the person mirrored being deceased.

Another related phenomenon he discusses is the *'Fantasy of Cyclical Living'*, wherein an individual expects certain catastrophic events to recur whenever an event arises within a temporal cycle. A striking example of an imposed mythology occurs when a sibling dies and the parents, either consciously or unconsciously, equate or merge both children.

Pollock also provides a compelling example drawn from the life of Vincent van Gogh. Van Gogh was a replacement child, named exactly after his dead predecessor, and frequently passed by his brother's tombstone, where he would see their shared name. He was born one year later, on the same day and in the same month as his deceased sibling. He was recorded in the register of births under the same number as his brother, 29. Vincent van Gogh died by suicide in 1890, on July 29th.

The personal myth and story thus contain both unconscious and conscious content. They are lived and carried out, in most circumstances, unbeknownst to the person. In cases where the individual is aware of a drama being enacted by them, they are almost never aware of the full extent to which this personal narrative has influenced their life. It would also appear that self-damaging narratives tend to be unconsciously actuated, whereas positive and self-edifying narratives are more consciously directed.

This is logical, since the individual who possesses sufficient self-awareness has, with the right tools, the capacity to seize the reins of their destiny and create a life in harmony with their ideals. Such is the goal of psychoanalysis: to foster self-awareness, thereby enabling one to discover the strength that previously lay dormant within and to allow it to manifest properly, authoring a more authentic and purposeful life.

In truth, we are all the authors of our own stories. Now,

with what tools do we compose these stories? With what ink and paper do we create the romances, tragedies, and heroic victories of our own tale?

The Tarot. Indeed, its scenes are like fragments of stories that individuals can piece together to compose themselves and their personal narratives. What makes the Tarot unique is that these are symbols that already exist within the individual, both projective and interpretive, containing within themselves material already present — comprehensive enough to be relatable, yet abstract enough to be infinitely malleable to the internal world of the individual. The Tarot contains within itself collective memory and archetypal imagery while at the same time possessing a projective nature.

While in the Tarot we are indeed viewing the story of the Fool, we are also viewing the story of the Fool within ourselves. Vleminck (2010) writes about the significance of the story of Cain and Abel, particularly its clinical value in psychotherapy. He explores the *'Cain Complex'* and its relation to Oedipus, explaining how the story of Cain and Abel illuminates the Thanatic instinct (i.e. internal nature). In it, he refers to Szondi (1969/1973), writing beautifully: "In every Cain, there is an Abel... Cain is Abel before and after the murder." Before, due to his innocence; after, due to his repentance. The figure of Cain exists within every person as the sadistic impulse.

Thus, while the story of Oedipus illustrates the tragedy of self-knowledge, the story of Cain illustrates the tragedy of jealousy and hatred. Hughes (2007), who also wrote about Cain and Szondi's work, likewise stated: "In every Cain there is an Abel, and in every Abel a Cain." I would argue, then, that the story of Cain and Abel is less about Abel and more about Cain. It is fitting that it is always referred to as *"Cain and Abel"*, not *"Abel and Cain"*, for the main character is not Abel but rather his older brother.

This is not merely a narrative about a victim of jealousy and narcissistic rage; rather, it is the story of an individual who could not adequately confront the aspects of himself that he detested. As a result of his submission to primitive impulse, Cain suffered severe psychological consequences:

"My iniquity is greater than that I may deserve pardon. Behold, thou dost cast me out this day from the face of the earth, and I shall be hidden from thy face, and I shall be a vagabond and a fugitive on the earth: everyone, therefore, that findeth me shall kill me." (Douay-Rheims Bible, 1899/2003, Genesis 4:13–14).

Before this act of repentance, however, Cain, after having killed Abel, bathed in his blood. To bathe in the blood of one's dead victim implies a psychological and psychopathic element to the killing. At the time Cain slew his brother, it is assumed that there were no other humans on the planet save Adam, Eve, Cain, Abel, and their sisters, who would become their wives. Thus, it can be deduced that Cain was here referring to the ghost of Abel, who he feared would return as an avenging spirit (Hooke, 1939).

Dundes (2009) has argued that vampires and the fear of the undead are, in actuality, projections of the fear that the dearly departed will return to avenge wrongs committed against them in life by those still living. The fear in question is therefore a product of guilt.

The story of Cain is clearly a psychological one. Yet it is more than that; it is the characterisation of what exists within every individual, and its narrative represents psychoanalysis in its ancient and raw form — mythic storytelling.

With due reason, Freud (1908/1959) observed that analysands' speech often resembles mythological stories. Mythology and psychoanalysis are inseparably intertwined.

INTRODUCTION

Almost all psychoanalytic complexes are derived from archetypal and/or mythological figures: Narcissus (Freud, 1914/1957); Cain (Webb & Szondi, 1964); Oedipus (Freud, 1900/1953); Jocasta (Akhtar, 2009a); Medea (Akhtar, 2009b); Laius (Ross, 1982); the Madonna–Prostitute (Freud, 1912/1957); Electra (Akhtar, 2009c); Fortunata (Mairal, 2015); Don Juan (Eber, 1981); Don Quixote (Iniesta, 2011); Cassandra (Gigerenzer, 2014); Messiah (Gordillo et al., 2020); Peter Pan (Kiley, 1983); Romeo and Juliet (Gierczyk & Dobosz, 2022); Hercules (Berger, 2005, p. 82); Alexander (Meyer, 1989); Othello (Todd & Dewhurst, 1955); Lot (Polhemus, 2005); Napoleon (Knapen, Blaker, & Van Vugt, 2018); Cain, and Moses (Webb & Szondi, 1964), among many others.

Although some of these figures are products of myth and others of history, both function as symbols. These figures are real insofar as they exist within ourselves. Myths are the royal road to the intrapsychic world, for the unconscious reveals itself as a mythological unconscious (De Vleminck, 2013). Venus' vision of Adonis' death represents the maternal anxiety that arises as a mother witnesses her son's growing beauty and its implications for his sexual independence and eventual abandonment of her, an attachment anxiety rooted in sexual envy (Kahn, 1981; Rebhorn, 1979).

Man created myth in order to psychoanalyse himself. **The Tarot is myth**, and in the same way that the aforementioned myths exist within us, so too does the Tarot. Case (1920) wrote: "Through the study of the Tarot, we can gain insights into the workings of our own minds, uncovering the patterns and beliefs that shape our experiences. This awareness is the first step towards healing and personal growth." Within us exists the heartbreak of the Three of Swords or the regret of the Five of Cups.

Myths provide meaning and structure to life (Anastopoulos et al., 2010); thus, by becoming aware of these symbols within ourselves, we can understand the underlying psychological processes that drive our emotions and behaviours. This awareness allows us to confront these aspects of our psyche, leading to greater self-awareness and psychological growth. By exploring these archetypal symbols, we engage in a process of self-reflection and healing, uncovering the hidden parts of ourselves that influence our thoughts and actions. This journey of self-discovery is crucial for achieving a balanced and harmonious inner world, ultimately enabling us to navigate life's challenges with a deeper understanding of our own inner workings.

The understanding of the cards is therefore the mythologising of oneself, a process that occurs within psychoanalysis. Anastopoulos et al., (2010) identified that myths play an integral role in therapy and in the life of the adolescent. He stated that myths provide answers to life through their exposition of ideals, social values, traditional beliefs, and their metaphysical, cosmological, sociological, and psychological natures. It may be through this faculty that the Tarot possesses a predictive nature, for since it is myth, these same premises also apply to it.

Consciousness searches for meaning, and myth articulates meaning (Anastopoulos et al., 2010). This meaning is solidified through the manifestation of a symbol. Dundes (1980) defines a symbol as a meaningful unit that represents or stands for something else, often an abstract concept or a set of interrelated concepts.

Referring to dreams, Freud (1900/2010) stated that "a symbol in a dream stands for a repressed desire, and the process of interpretation is essentially a process of translating symbols back into the underlying unconscious wishes." Klein (1930) wrote, "Symbols are the vehicles through which the child attempts to understand and gain control over internal and external reality."

Thus, when we synthesise these meanings through a psychoanalytic lens, a symbol emerges as a collaboration between the conscious and the unconscious. It is an enigma, a concealed truth that invites silent contemplation and profound experience. A symbol unites the known with the unknown, the repressed with the conscious, and fantasy with reality. It is the midpoint between the psychic and the physical.

Ricoeur (1969/1974) defines a symbol as having a double meaning: a literal, surface definition, and a deeper, underlying significance. Interpretation allows one to penetrate the surface meaning and uncover the profound one. The interpretation of symbols therefore permits insightful realisations.

Rancour-Laferriere (2018) analysed devotion to the Blessed Virgin Mary from a psychoanalytic perspective and opined that Oedipal feelings towards one's biological mother are sublimated and transformed into love for the heavenly mother, who is spotless and immaculate. The fiery Oedipal love is thus kindled and transformed into a more perfect spiritual love for Mother Mary.

I have likewise analysed the symbolism and devotion of the Sacred Heart of Jesus in a similar manner (de Justin, 2024). Noticeable among clergy but equally applicable to the laity, passionate and romantic feelings directed towards another person are displaced onto the Sacred Heart, so that the nun who has sworn her chastity to God the Father and has been espoused to God the Son may engage in a romantic, affectionate, and passionate relationship with Christ, free from any carnality.

Fortune (1930) has also mentioned a similar phenomenon concerning nuns and priests who have been visited by angelic lovers. I recall to mind *The Ecstasy of Santa Teresa*, where she testified:

"I saw in [the hand of the angel] a long spear of gold, and at the end of the iron tip I seemed to see a point of fire. With this he seemed to pierce my heart several times so that it penetrated to my entrails. When he drew it out, I thought he was drawing them out with it, and he left me completely afire with a great love of God... The pain was so sharp that *it made me utter several moans, and so excessive was the sweetness caused me by this intense pain* (my emphasis) that one can never wish to lose it, nor will one's soul be content with anything less than God." (1565/2008)

Because symbols exist halfway between psychic and physical reality, they act as doorways into the deeper dimensions of the mind. For this reason, we can easily comprehend how the understanding of symbols leads to self-illumination. In ancient times, contemplation of the universe facilitated contemplation of the self, as individuals projected their essence onto the vast cosmos.

Astrology is a reflection of the self upon the starry sky, encapsulated by the words: "The heavens shew forth the glory of God, and the firmament declareth the work of his hands. Day to day uttereth speech, and night to night sheweth knowledge" (Psalm 18:2-3, Douay-Rheims). The affairs and conflicts of the gods were representations of our own struggles and experiences. Through myth, humanity sought to explain and understand itself.

Man projected his aggressivity onto Mars, sensuality onto Venus, emotionality onto Luna, and his sense of self onto the Sun; hence, the Sun is the centre of our universe. However, as man became enlightened by science, he ceased to perceive within himself the celestial Adam and no longer saw the throne of God in the heavens. A profound disconnection thus occurred. We lost touch with the gods and, in turn, with the deepest parts of our own being.

This severance from the divine and the cosmic order led to a diminished understanding of ourselves and our place in the universe. Symbols in the past possessed greater existential and emotional significance than they do now. They nonetheless continue to exist today, though many people acknowledge them only unconsciously. I do not believe that the common American is aware of the identity of the woman in the Statue of Liberty, despite the monument having been visited by 81,082,542 people since 2000 (National Park Service [NPS], 2024). What we have today is the consequence of science.

By functioning as doorways to the psychological world, symbols, particularly those to which we are emotionally attached, illuminate our internal reality and lead us towards self-illumination. This principle of self-illumination and realisation is also known as *anagnorisis*.

Anagnorisis, in Aristotle's *Poetics*, means discovery or recognition. In virtually all psychotherapy, the therapist guides the client towards self-discovery and recognition of the forces within. Topographically, this process involves bringing the unconscious closer to consciousness. Freud (1933/1964) described this structurally and succinctly when he said, "Where Id was, there shall Ego be." This means that the consciousness of the Ego will come to recognise what lies hidden within the Id.

Hence the words of Christ: "For there is nothing covered, that shall not be revealed; neither hid, that shall not be known. Therefore whatsoever ye have spoken in darkness shall be heard in the light, and that which ye have spoken in the ear in closets shall be proclaimed upon the housetops." (Luke 12:2–3, KJV).

In his exposition of literary and poetic tragedy, Aristotle writes that *anagnorisis* is the change from ignorance to knowledge. In psychoanalysis, the individual moves from ignorance of their condition to awareness of their psychic reality and acceptance of themselves. Rizq (2022) notes that the etymology of the root "ana-" implies a retroactive effect, a learning of what was already known or available.

Thus, the client is not learning anything new, but rather becoming aware of what was already latent. Freud established this with Breuer (1893/1955), concretising the task of therapy as being the bring forth of catharsis through the doctor's suggestion or by the arousal of memories and ideas associated with the repressed affect. This process can be tragic, illuminating, or both.

Rizq refers to Cave's (1988) literary analysis of *anagnorisis*, who specifies that what is discovered is almost always a part of the individual — "the birthmark, the scar, the casket, the handbag": aspects of the person's identity. In Longus' *Daphnis and Chloe*, the articles found with the infants are later revealed to connect them to the royal family, and they are subsequently wed. In the Oedipus legend, his mother is revealed to be the Queen, the source of his own person and identity.

In *Sleeping Beauty*, the tragedy of the tale depends upon Princess Aurora's *anagnorisis*: after discovering her royal nobility, she is heartbroken and falls into despair upon realising that the man she fell in love with will never be able to see her again, since she was in reality a princess arranged at birth to be married to Prince Philip. Aurora literally awakens from unconsciousness to discover that the man she met in the forest is the same prince who rescued her. Both *Sleeping Beauty* and *Oedipus* contain the tragic element of *anagnorisis* that was expected to be positive but is instead ironically negative.

Fortunata and Jacinta: The History of Two Married Women

also contains *anagnorisis* throughout the novel and perhaps portrays it in a manner more compatible with the modern age. Fortunata initially believes that her passionate love affair with Juanito Santa Cruz will eventually lead him to leave his wife, Jacinta (also his cousin), for her. She clings to the idea that she is his true love and that their connection is stronger than any marital bond.

This belief is central to her actions throughout much of the novel. Fortunata's *anagnorisis* comes when she finally understands that Juanito will never truly commit to her. This realisation occurs after Juanito's lack of emotional stability, perceived betrayals, and her recognition of the cyclical nature of their relationship, in which he continually returns to Jacinta, leaving Fortunata in mortal despair.

Jacinta, on the other hand, enters her marriage to Juanito Santa Cruz with the belief that she can maintain a happy and fulfilling life with him. She initially ignores or underestimates the significance of Juanito's affair with Fortunata, whom she regards as merely a fleeting conquest, believing that her love and dedication will ultimately prevail. Jacinta's *anagnorisis* begins to unfold as she becomes increasingly aware of the depth of Juanito's involvement with Fortunata. This awareness is not immediate but grows gradually as she confronts the reality of her husband's infidelity and the impact it has on their marriage and the lives of those involved, revealing a greater consequence that had previously been unknown.

In *Amarte Así*, the story centres on Ignacio's eventual realisation that the man with whom he shared a tender relationship as a little boy is, in fact, his father, a truth known to almost all the other characters. Eve's *anagnorisis* occurs in the Garden of Eden, where she learns "Good and Evil". *El Clon* involves the *anagnorisis* of Daniel, who discovers that he is both the clone of Lucas and the reincarnation of his twin brother Diego. The story of *Hansel and Gretel* revolves around their discovery that their stepmother intends to abandon them in the forest, and that their father is complicit in the act.

All of these stories involve characters discovering a deeper, often tragic, truth about their identities or circumstances. These revelations force them to confront aspects of their lives or selves that had been hidden, repressed, or misunderstood. Just as these characters come to terms with significant, often painful truths about themselves, so too does the psychoanalytic patient gradually uncover repressed or unconscious material. This revelation is essential for personal growth and transformation, much like the characters' realisations, which propel their stories forward, sometimes with tragic consequences.

Vleminck (2010), with reason, states that the legend of Oedipus depicts the tragedy of human self-knowledge: painful yet necessary. Self-discovery in psychoanalysis shares profound similarities with the concept of literary tragedy, both in structure and in emotional impact. As said before, life is a theatre and we are its actors and scriptwriters, so it is no surprise that the laws of literature apply to life and psychology as well.

In classical tragedy, the protagonist undergoes a journey that leads to a dramatic moment of recognition or *anagnorisis*, where hidden truths about themselves or their circumstances are revealed. This moment, while transformative, often results in the protagonist's downfall, bringing about a profound change in their life and identity. Similarly, the process of psychoanalysis guides individuals toward self-discovery, gradually unveiling repressed or unconscious material. The confrontation with these buried aspects of the psyche can be as painful and destabilising as the tragic hero's realisation of their fate.

Central to both tragedy and psychoanalysis is the role of conflict and suffering. In tragedy, the protagonist's internal and external struggles lead to suffering, culminating in a catastrophic awareness of their flaws or the inevitability of their fate. In psychoanalysis, the therapeutic process involves confronting internal conflicts, such as repressed desires or unresolved traumas, leading to psychological suffering. However, this suffering is seen as necessary for personal growth, paralleling how tragedy uses suffering to achieve catharsis and insight.

Aristotle's notion of catharsis, where the audience experiences emotional purification through the protagonist's journey, finds a parallel in the cathartic release experienced by the patient in psychoanalysis. The emotional liberation that comes from processing repressed emotions mirrors the emotional cleansing that tragedy provides its audience. According to Freud and Breuer (1893/1955), catharsis is a reaction of the blocked emotions and by this means of bringing about their catharsis and their discharge.

Moreover, both tragedy and psychoanalysis share a sense of the inevitability of certain outcomes. In tragedy, the protagonist is often powerless against their fate, driven by a tragic flaw or predetermined destiny. While psychoanalysis does not propose a predetermined fate, it acknowledges the powerful influence of unconscious drives on an individual's life. The therapeutic journey involves recognising these unconscious forces, much like the tragic hero's belated realisation of the powers leading to their demise.

Finally, the duality of enlightenment and suffering is a key aspect of both tragedy and psychoanalysis. In tragedy, the protagonist often achieves a form of self-awareness through suffering, but this awareness comes at a great cost, heightening the poignancy of their downfall. Similarly, in psychoanalysis, self-discovery leads to a deeper understanding of oneself, yet this enlightenment often involves recognising painful truths and confronting past mistakes. It is Mary Magdalene, the weeping and tragic woman, who discovers the resurrected Christ in the tragic narrative of St Mark's Gospel (Jay, 2014) and proclaims the divine revelation, 'I have seen the Lord' (John 20:18 KJV). Jay also points out that the element of tragic recognition lies within the crucifixion itself – the failure of the Jews and the crowd to recognise Jesus as God the Son, his eventual death, and the subsequent divine consequences: the darkening of the sky, solar eclipse, earthquake, and the demolition of the Jewish temple. The therapeutic journey, like the tragic narrative, is one of moving through suffering towards a more integrated and self-aware state of being, where enlightenment is achieved, albeit at significant emotional and psychological cost. In both domains, the journey toward self-discovery is essential for personal transformation, even as it reveals the inherent sorrows and complexities of the human condition.

Suffering is central to self-awareness. Psychoanalysis (and consequently, self-analysis) involves understanding the significance of suffering and recognising powerful emotional experiences as well as aspects of the self. Hughes (1979) wrote wonderfully: *'Whether one acts out Cain characteristics in the foreground or in the background, one is still responsible for the whole.'* The psychological task that individuals must undertake in order to mature is to become aware of the internal Cain. As I have personally defined here and in other works, complexes and myths exist in the psyche as living characters. They are roles that the fragmented aspects of the self interpret and enact. Cain and Abel live on in every one of us. Webb and Szondi (1964) expound a Cain–Moses striving within us all: the former referring to a drive to destroy, and the latter to a drive to control these emotions and project them onto that which is constructive. Thus, *'the Cain who lives among and inside us remains the same Cain that was once immortalised in the Bible and in sagas'* (De Vlemnick, 2013).

As a matter of fact, Cain and Abel are present in the Tarot. We find their depiction in the engraving on the bedside of the individual in the Nine of Swords. They are plagued by their repressed emotions (the inner Cain), and the subsequent guilt that arises leaves them in despair. It is in these particular ways that myths reveal themselves within each human individual, though in varying forms. The way Napoleon, Moses, Cain, and others reveal themselves will differ for every person. *Anagnorisis* involves removing the masks of these symbols and understanding their core for ourselves. We must comprehend how these symbols act and interact both intrapsychically and externally. All the dramas of life are caused by the interaction of one person's internal symbols with another's.

Hughes (2007) points out yet another crucial detail: the very duty of depth psychology is to know the *"unknowable"* unconscious. This knowledge (*anagnorisis*) is made possible via three languages:

1. **The Symptom:** Derived from repression and early childhood trauma, it informs psychoanalytic interpretation as the *"return of the repressed."* The symptom itself is symbolic.
2. **The Symbol:** Erupting from the archetypes of Jung, symbols return mainly in dreams. Jung noted that ancestral traits become buried in the unconscious and are passed down through generations.
3. **Language of Choice:** A selection of possibilities inherited from the familial

unconscious. Szondi, who complemented both Jung and Freud, regarded this as explaining why there are families of lawyers, doctors, cooks, etc. This may also account for why cheating fathers raise cheating sons (Havlíček et al., 2011) or why there sometimes appears to be, within a family, a lineage of men with Don Juanism.

As pointed out, symbols are the method by which the unconscious becomes conscious. They are the means by which it manifests, the door through which the conscious mind may enter and leave. Archetypal and mythological symbols are the pinnacle of psychic language, for they are not only the images of feeling and of being, but of existence and the human condition itself. The Rider–Waite–Smith Tarot, as a set of symbols, equally archetypal, mythological, philosophical, and emotional, is a tool for *Anagnorisis*.

Why is the Rider–Waite–Smith Tarot distinguished from other modern versions? Because all modern versions derive their symbolism, whether critically or admiringly, from this deck. It contains multidimensional, emotional, philosophical, mythic, symbolic, and literary references which appeal to the unconscious in manifold ways. Its symbols reach the unconscious through every pore, allowing all facets of the psyche to be touched, insofar as the individual is able to investigate them. The language of the unconscious is symbolism. Thus, the cards become the alphabet of the unconscious. Their illustrations are deliberately daunting and thought-provoking.

Hidden symbols and illustrative elements lie within every card, to the extent that, with each meditation upon a particular image, one is bound to discover new and concealed details. This profundity of intricacy and design is scarcely found in other decks, both prior to and after its conception. Its enduring popularity among all other decks is very likely due to its profound resonance with the collective unconscious of the masses.

There have been some who posit that a psychoanalytic lens is not constructive for Tarot (Auger, 2004). The contrary has clearly been established and shall continue to be for the duration of this work. A psychoanalytic examination of the Tarot reveals previously unmentioned insights, including some that remain inaccessible through other interpretive frameworks. These include the betrayal of defence mechanisms, idealisations, splitting, identification, magical thought, death anxiety, annihilation anxiety, existence, weakness, phantasies of omnipotence, archaic images, universal values (Anastopoulos, 2010), ego development, the pleasure principle, the reality principle, complexes, intrapsychic structures, repetition compulsion, symbolic substitution, displacement, psychic reality, and external reality. All of these shall be demonstrated in subsequent chapters.

Indeed, I have not seen a psychoanalytic interpretation of the Tarot as profound as this treatise. A psychoanalytic examination reveals that the Tarot is not only a spiritual tool but a psychological one as well. The content of our unconscious desires expresses itself in a magnified way through myth (in this case, Tarot), which, conversely, appeals to every individual due to its psychic resonance. Hence, it can be used to solve problems and explore solutions.

Freud's emphasis on the symbolic nature of religious myths can encourage a deeper symbolic analysis of Tarot cards, seeing them not merely as tools for divination but as windows into the deeper, hidden layers of the psyche. Through a psychoanalytic framework, one can interpret the Tarot cards as representations of unconscious desires, conflicts, and repressed material. For example, the Devil card may reveal repressed instincts and desires that seek expression, while the Hierophant card, associated with religious authority and tradition, represents the introjected authority of cultural and religious norms.

The following chapters will no doubt demonstrate the value of the Tarot for clinical, analytic, and personal use. As with all tools, there are those that work well for some and not so for others. Clearly, for individuals with psychosis, schizophrenia, or delusional disorders, the condition of problematic magical thinking and the blending of psychic and external reality make Tarot integration deleterious. The mental health practitioner, however, shall be able to discern the healthy use of the Tarot within their sessions. It is an excellent tool when therapy has reached a plateau or when deeper, refreshing insights into the self are desired. It is likewise effective for discovering new material for analysis.

For the curious mental health practitioner, I highly suggest experiencing the Tarot as a means of personal exploration for yourself before offering the experience to others. Once experienced personally, its efficacy shall doubtlessly be defended and more openly examined within the realm of psychological science. It is my hope that this work propels such movement.

❧ 1 ☙
PSYCHOSEXUAL DEVELOPMENT & THE TAROT AS THE JOURNEY OF THE CHILD

Psychosexual development begins at conception *(Berenbaum & Beltz, 2011; Moore, Persaud, & Torchia, 2020; Swaab, 2004)*. The psychological and emotional environment of the parents, particularly their unconscious desires and fantasies, may begin to shape the child's psyche even before birth. Likewise, both mother and child share a transfusion of hormones within their symbiotic relationship. The neurochemicals produced within the mother are subsequently transmitted to the child. The thoughts of the mother and child are also shared.

It has been suggested that this phenomenon, known as *embryonic telepathy* (Cheek 1992a), occurs when the thoughts of mother and child are mutually influential. The mother's thoughts can influence the physiological and physical condition of the child (for example, producing movements, miscarriage, or other responses). Conversely, the child's needs *in utero* may be transmitted to the mother through thoughts and images (for example, cravings or action-oriented impulses).

Cheek (1992b) examined the influence of embryonic memories on adults, particularly in relation to their interpersonal relationships with their parents. He found that *'permanent unconscious memory could occur for an embryo at the time its mother is told she is pregnant'* (p. 5).

This means that it is possible the psychic relationship between mother and child is established when the mother becomes aware of his existence within her. The official infusion of psychic energy may begin at this point. A woman may believe that she is pregnant, but due to the emotional tumult created when the diagnosis is made official, maternal fear or anger may surge and profoundly influence the embryo. This is clearly one of the primary psychic infusions on the part of the mother.

In response, the embryonic child (I use the term *embryonic child* because, psychically, it is indeed a child) will feel confused, for it expects its mother to be happy. Upon receiving both neurochemical and psychological impressions of fear, doubt, and stress (such as cortisol), the next reaction will almost invariably be a sense of rejection. Cheek notes that the embryo (or foetus) is typically aware that its incubator is subconsciously happy to be pregnant if her environment is a joyful one. Confusion arises, however, when it receives an influx of distress signals from the mother.

Cheek likewise emphasises that 'It is important in therapy to bring this repressed information into *conscious awareness [my emphasis]* in a reframing process' (p. 6). The conceptus responds to maternal distress with great alarm, interpreting her emotions as signals of rejection or even abandonment. This early misinterpretation can cause lasting harm, which may later be exacerbated by subsequent traumas.

Szondi (1956/2011) even suggested that the mother may

influence the appearance of her child if she fantasises or idealises the image of another individual, or her own mental image. This phenomenon of psychic impression has also been recorded in numerous other circumstances.

When a pregnant mother was working in a hayfield, her husband threw at her a young hare he had found in the hay; it struck her on the cheek and neck. Her daughter was born with, on the left cheek, an oblong patch of soft dark hair, in both colour and character clearly resembling the fur of a very young hare (Mackay et al., 1891).

In another circumstance, a lady who was pregnant became much interested in a story in which one of the characters possessed a supernumerary digit, and this image often recurred to her mind. Her baby was born with a supernumerary digit on one hand (Jenkyns, 1895).

When pregnant, a mother saw in the forest a newborn fawn that bore two heads. When she gave birth, her own child was born with two heads (Hartmann, 1895).

A pregnant woman once traumatically witnessed a child run over by a streetcar, which crushed the upper and back part of its head. Her own child was born anencephalic and acranial, with an entire absence of the vault of the skull (Stahl, 1896).

In Cuba, there is a common belief that a pregnant woman should not store cash in her bra or allow it to press upon her skin, lest she desire that the face printed on the note should appear on her newborn.

This may explain why, in cases of infidelity, though the child may appear to be the husband's, it is not. During pregnancy, there is a revolution of psychical energy. Even if the father is a tertiary figure within the mother–child dyad, he likewise participates in the libidinal drama through his *couvade syndrome*, whereby pseudo-pregnancy symptoms are experienced by him (for example, bloating, cravings, headaches, mood swings, hormonal changes, and weight gain).

I argue, however, for a much earlier commencement of the infusion of psychic energy. Although I concur that pregnancy involves an intense psychological enactment and influence upon all members of the family, I do not believe it is the first instance in which the conceptus receives libidinal cathexis from his parents. Rather, I posit that this process of emotional investment begins even before the parents are adults themselves, indeed, even when they themselves are born.

The pregnancy wishes of the parent as a child may just as well create the psychic foundations for the perceptual existence of their future child later on. Biological instincts, experience, and education combine in childhood to prepare a child to become a parent in the future. This concept is explored and enacted in the wish for a child. These wishes may concretise the unconscious (or conscious) expectations of the future child and thus behave as a sort of reservoir for future projections. In other words, these fantasies create a psychic template that influences the child's psychosexual development even pre-conception.

It could also be suggested that the unresolved psychosexual issues or desires of the parents, or even ancestors, are transmitted intergenerationally to the embryonic child. The parents' desires and anxieties about the child (what they wish for the child to be, what they fear, whether it will remind them of rival siblings, disliked in-laws, parents, etc.) could be internalised by the foetus (later child), forming the basis for their later psychosexual development.

As mentioned earlier, the article by Cheek implied that the psychic energy and investment of the parent in the child may begin once the mother is aware of the embryo within her. However, I would like to posit an alternative, complementary view: that the infusion and investment of psychic energy begins before the parents even unite. In reality, this infusion and investment of psychic energy occurs during childhood and genitality.

A woman is born with a fixed number of eggs for the entirety of her life. This implies that the child who is to be born to her in the future already partially exists within her. Thus, the psychic energy that is created during the pregnancy wishes of the little girl may direct itself towards this very egg, to later be adapted and, of course, fertilised by a sperm. Hence, the child, in his inchoate, ovular existence, is receiving libidinal energy from his mother even when she herself is still a child.

Boys likewise have pregnancy wishes (Jacobson, 1950), and the same principle can be applied to them as well. At birth, the testes of a biological male do not contain sperm, but do indeed contain immature stem cells that can produce spermatozoa after puberty. Once puberty begins, signals from the pituitary gland instruct the testes to start producing the hormone testosterone, and the testes begin to increase in size. The first ejaculation occurs, and the process of sperm production and seminal elimination is initiated. Thus, the pregnancy wishes of the child and their corresponding libidinal energy may also direct themselves onto the spermatic existence of the male child (future father). The only difference with male involvement in this process is that the sperm undergo a continuous cycle of elimination and regeneration within the genitals.

Thus, psychic investment could perhaps only be transmitted during insemination. This may connect to Freud's (1898) position that *coitus interruptus* (where ejaculation occurs outside the vagina to avoid conception) may lead to psychological disturbances. Because the highest pleasurable state of orgasm is frustrated, a form of sexual repression occurs, preventing the full expression of sexual satisfaction. The complete discharge of tension is, as the name suggests, interrupted; through masturbation, the libidinal energy associated with orgasm is only partially released and partially dammed up. Satisfaction is acknowledged, but full gratification remains unachieved, leading to the accumulation of tension.

Thus, the investment of psychic energy on the part of the man, though its psychical foundations are established in childhood, may indeed only be transferred during insemination. The woman, as the passive and receptive component of conception, already has both foundation and transmission established.

And what of the case of abortion? The *conceptus* (psychic child) is killed, and this structure of libidinal cathexis (emotional investment) is destroyed. In both intentional and unintentional abortions, however, each individual retains within themselves the reservoir of psychic energy and the templates necessary to regenerate another psychic child, should they choose to do so.

ORALITY

Orality commences roughly between the ages of 0 to 2. This is the stage wherein oral sexuality is predominant, and all libidinal energy is invested in oral activity. This epoch in the child's life is marked by a special attachment to the mother as the provider of oral satisfaction.

Thus, having established the embryonic and pre-conception existence of the child, we arrive at the tarot. The singular card which has the right, honour, and virtue to be called embryonic and pre-conception in relation to the entire deck is *The Fool*.

The Fool, numbered at 0, represents neither beginning nor end, but the spark of creation. Life begins with The Fool. *It is the child who has been brought into the world from the darkness of the womb into the light of the world.* It represents the embryonic child coming out of the womb and seeing the light of the world, the light of day, the brightness of the hospital lights (hence the shining sun beaming down). With just reason, the sun is only depicted on one other card, The Sun card, which correspondingly portrays a child riding a horse.

The anxiety of birth (Rank, 1929/1993) and the traumatic birth situation are represented by a precarious precipice which The Fool, though beholding the beauty and vastness of the world, is sure to fall from. There are rugged mountains in the background of The Fool card. The vagina is likewise rugged and layered; therefore, The Fool is the embryonic child, beholding his entryway into the world via the vaginal canal and seeing the light at the end of the tunnel.

The dog, as the only other character so close to The Fool (embryo) in proximity, represents the placenta as co-host of the womb. The placenta's role in the imagery of The Fool is especially relevant regarding birth trauma. The Fool's precarious position, as mentioned, represents the anxiety of birth, the moment when the child is severed from the placenta (the dog) and must begin to rely on other forms of sustenance and support. The child experiences separation from the womb as a falling sensation (Pattnaik & Al Khalili, 2025) hence The Fool falling from the cliff. The dog's presence indicates the lingering attachment to this source of life, and the anxiety of losing this connection could be the first unconscious trauma that shapes the child's psychosexual development.

The dog is barking and white in colour, which could likewise be a reference to the doctors dressed in their white coats coaching both mother and child during the delivery. Even Waite (1959) considers the psychological dimension of the tarot when he says regarding The Fool, "His wallet is inscribed with dim signs to show that many subconscious memories are stored up in the soul."

The following card, which is The Fool as student and illumined, is The Magician. This is *the Id in full and pure representation*. The creative master and master of the world around him, his world is shaped by the magical force within him that governs love and hate, creation and destruction. This is the reservoir of all creativity and the form of creation in both the future and the present.

In his hand, he holds a magic wand. This is the phallus which he so proudly bears, as well as a symbol of his omnipotence fantasies. Before him, he holds the instruments of the four elements: Cups, Wands, Swords, and Pentacles. These represent the environment that obeys the will and caprice of the child. His every need is magically satisfied, for he is a magician. With one cry, one magic utterance, one spell, he is at once attended to by all those around him, frantically and urgently.

These magical instruments also represent his own creativity. The flowers before him, roses and lilies, signify the infantile and sexual nature of this entity: simultaneously infantile (lilies) and passionate (roses). He points downwards, for everything proceeds from the Id. It is a gesture of indication. Around his belt is a serpent (a hidden symbol) consuming itself. This serpent is a symbol of the unconscious, the domain of the Id.

Above his head is the symbol of infinity, which pictorially appears as two breasts. The infant's source of life and survival, no longer being the placenta, is now the mother's breast, and is oriented towards them.

The High Priestess is the pre-Oedipal mother. Water flows from her because she is the fount of wisdom and of life. Her breast milk is the sustenance that the child needs and hence is his life: "As newborn babes, desire the rational milk without guile, that thereby you may grow unto salvation" (1 Peter 2:2 DRV). The pomegranate has always been a sexual symbol. These round, red objects can represent the breast, but they are open, also representing the inside of the vulva and the vaginal canal, red and life-producing. Upon her head she bears a crown, a symbol of the mother's authority and omnipotence. In her hands she holds the Torah, the law, which is all the wisdom the child needs and desires. The moon is her footstool, for she is the first notion of God for the child. About her are two pillars, Boaz and Jachin, representing her two arms with which she cradles her child. The High Priestess thus represents the mother with her child at her breast.

ANALITY

The next phase of the child's development is the Anal phase, which occurs after the Oral phase, between the ages of two and four. In this stage, the child's libido is directed towards anal activity, such as toilet training. This stage is divided into two minor stages: anal-retentive and anal-expulsive. Future attitudes towards money are influenced by this stage (Freud, 1908/1959). This is represented extremely well by both the cards and, especially, the suit to follow.

The anal-retentive stage is represented by the Four of Pentacles (paranoid, retaining, stingy, hoarding, meticulous). Adults who have a libidinal fixation at the anal-retentive level are characterised by meticulousness, orderliness, rigidity, and frugality (Freud, 1908/1959). This behaviour is linked to infantile experiences in which, either to avoid harsh treatment or out of anger, the child held onto their faeces to prevent making a mess or to delay their parents' schedule. The man in the Four of Pentacles is thus an adult-child, accurately representing his internal nature and personality. Interestingly, this man sits on a chair or stool, clearly representing the toilet. This symbolises the child who, out of anger, retains his faeces and refuses to expel them. To further corroborate this, at his feet the man is supported by two pentacles, which unconsciously represent the booster footstools that children are given when they sit on the toilet. He is looking either towards the viewer or just beside them, as if stubbornly watching his parents who are waiting for him. The castles, towns, and fortresses behind him are his psychic defences made manifest, the embodiment of his need to hold onto what he has, whether it be wealth, faeces, security, or control over his environment. They are his unconscious attempt to protect himself from the fear of loss and the anxiety that accompanies it, reflecting the deep-seated, unresolved conflicts of the anal-retentive stage. It is worth noting that anal-retentive adults often report issues related to constipation (Freud, 1908/1959; Abraham, 1921/1927; Yilmatz et al., 2019). He wears a crown, but it is not a crown of nobility. The child at the anal stage is not as omnipotent as he was during orality, but he remains prioritised. The anal stage involves the degradation of external influence.

The Six of Pentacles, alternatively, represents the anal phase when expulsive (giving, reconcilable). With due reason, the Four of Pentacles precedes the Sixth, for in the same manner that four precedes six, so too does the anal-retentive stage precede the anal-expulsive. I have correlated the anal-expulsive phase with the Six of Pentacles, firstly through the anal phase's correspondences with money, and secondly because the child perceives his faeces as gifts he gives to his caregiver. In *the Six of Pentacles*, we see a man freely giving money to a beggar. Above him hang six pentacles. On his left, he holds a scale, which he raises above another beggar. These are the two parents to whom the child now happily bestows his gifts. The child is benevolent both with money and with his faeces. The defensive retention of the former stage is now overcome, for this scene takes place not within the fortress (defences), but rather outside the city walls, as seen in the background.

The reader may perhaps wonder why I did not proceed with *The Emperor* but instead turned towards the Minor Arcana. This is because the Tarot is a set of symbols, and as such, they are unifications and organisations of different psychological events. Those who oppose my perspective of the book for being 'unlinear' will in fact see that it is quite linear when the connections are made. This is further nourished by the links that exist between the Minor and Major Arcana, for there are indeed references to the Major Arcana within the Minor. This will be established later on.

PHALLICITY & OEDIPALITY

The phallic phase, occurring roughly between 4–6, contains within itself an entire sequence of cards, for it is indeed a theatre play in itself. It represents the height of the psychosexual drama of the individual and, hence, is composed of numerous cards and characters. Within it unfolds a plethora of actions and events, including, of course, the Oedipus complex, wherein the boy competes with his father for sexual domination of the mother.

The phallic child is the *Page of Wands*, now mastering the abilities of his penis, urinating with his hands, masturbating, and feeling proud of this source of pleasure. He is romantic and idealising (as indicated by his posture), and from this idealisation and romanticism is born the Oedipus complex. The three pyramids in the *Page of Wands* allude to the significance of the number three, as mentioned before (mother, father, child), as well as to the oedipal situation.

The Oedipus complex is represented by *The Lovers* card. It is the son and mother as mates in the Garden of Pleasure. Between them is a mountain, for in reality this fantasy would be an obstacle to fulfil, given the actual circumstances of the child. Above them is an archangel of light, representing the emergence of the unconscious into the light of day, but also the superego, which has permitted this, rather than prohibiting it, to take place. There are superego proto-forms before its official concretisation during phallicity, as Klein (2002) observed. The tree of life as the burning fruit behind the child represents his passions for the mother. The serpent lurking behind the mother is the incest taboo. This card is a depiction of Adam and Eve; thus, the serpent likewise can signify the participation of the mother on her behalf with the oedipal fantasy, which does indeed unconsciously occur (Laplanche, 1999). *The Lovers* as a name is obvious for the love that is felt between them. He admires her, for she has been the source of life and care for him thus far. She, all the while, admires the tall archangel, for her commitment still remains with a threatening and much larger male figure.

The Emperor is an overwhelmingly masculine image. It represents the father as an ideal, strong and powerful, bearing both a sceptre (penis) and globe (testicles) as a testament to his power. He is bearded, as a father figure. His number in the Arcana is 4. He sits on a throne that bears four rams, a symbol of the masculine principle, Mars and Aries. The very icon of Mars, an arrow pointing diagonally upward, is a phallic representation of the erect penis. The rugged mountains behind him are his domain. As mentioned, the rugged mountains in *The Fool* represented the inside of the vagina. Thus, *The Emperor* is the true owner of the mother's vagina, she being subject to his sexual demands. Waite reluctantly provides this signification when he says that *The Emperor* and *The Empress* represent married life. The water passing behind him is again a sexually phallic symbol, representing semen as it comes out of the urethra and flows through the mountains (vaginal cavity). In Waite's (1959) own words, "he represents virile power."

His sceptre is a long vertical rod with a horizontal bar at the top, crowned with a sphere. Mendel (1949) identified the vertical line as representing the father and the penis, the horizontal line as representing the vagina and femininity, and the circle as the mother and the womb.

The sceptre of *The Emperor* is thus a representation of penile penetration into the mother's womb. Mendel points out that the Athenian man drew the letter *t* as an equilateral cross, rather than in the Roman style, which features a more elevated horizontal bar. He interprets this as a manifestation of the bisexuality of Athenian men. For *The Emperor*, his sceptre is not at all bisected but rather sits entirely at the tip. Notice how the Emperor bears not a sword but a sceptre. He is the post-oedipal father. He need not be minacious or castrating, for his authority is already acknowledged. The reason he bears a sceptre and not a sword is that he is not intent on killing his son. This is not an image of Laius. The sceptre and globe that the father bears shall be passed on to his son so that he may use them with his own wife rather than his mother.

The *King of Swords*, on the other hand, represents the father as castrating. Justly have I discerned the *King of Swords* as the image of Laius, for Laius was indeed a king. The Laius complex is the psychological organisation of the filicidal wishes of the father towards his son (Akhtar et al., 1995). The *King of Swords* sits on a throne adorned with fairies and butterflies. On his head he bears a crown with the image of a cherub. His cape is dark, in contrast to the *Queen of Swords*, whose gown reflects the heavens. Additionally, there are two birds in the sky, compared to a singular one in the *Queen of Swords*. He bears his sword upright. Unlike the *Knight of Swords*, the king knows how to wield his much larger penis. Notice how the *King of Swords* bears no armour or shield. He is threatened by his much younger, stronger, and sexually virile and attractive son. The erect positioning of the sword, of course, represents the erect paternal penis. Thus, he will, at any moment if needed, castrate and kill his younger competitor in order to protect the earth over which he has domain, earth representing the mother's body (Klein, 2002).

The Empress represents the oedipal mother, seductive, sensual, and gratifying. She lies on luxurious pillows and is adorned in luscious garments. By her side is her shield, which bears the yonic symbol of Venus. This shield is in the shape of a heart, representing love. Her robes are adorned with pomegranates, a symbol of her breasts and vulva. She holds a small sceptre or wand in her hand, representative of the child's small penis compared to the enormous sword or phallus of the father. Behind her is earth, the symbol of her body. From behind her flows a river that reaches her feet.

Pamela Colman Smith was heavily inspired by Shakespeare and represented his plays and characters through the Tarot. This river, as well as the entire scene, may be an allusion to Shakespeare's *Venus and Adonis*, wherein Venus herself tells Adonis: *"I'll be a park, and thou shalt be my deer. Feed where thou wilt, on mountain or in dale; Graze on my lips, and if those hills be dry, Stray lower, where the pleasant fountains lie."*

The *Empress* card itself is a sensual, romantic card. The embryonic waters flow and become not only symbolic of breast milk but, in this context and with more precision, female ejaculation as well. The entirety of the *Venus and Adonis* poem is saturated with imagery of greenery, gardens, and pastures. The *Empress* card, too, is the same. Corroborating this connection still further may be the presence of the wheat and pomegranate dress, symbolic of Proserpina. Allegedly, Venus and Proserpina battled over Adonis.

And what of the crown of twelve stars? The Roman Christian will undoubtedly recognise this as the crown of the Blessed Virgin Mary. What role, then, does Mary play in our interpretation? In *The High Priestess*, we saw a woman with a cross, the Torah, and a moon at her feet, all symbols of Mary, especially of the Immaculate Conception.

The lunar crown of *The High Priestess* may also be symbolic of Mary, who was equated with the Moon in early Christian beliefs and some cultural traditions (Ihnat, 2016). Yet here, *The Empress* wears a crown of twelve stars. Is this figure Mary, Proserpina, or Venus? Dear reader, she is all.

The mother during the oedipal period is indulgent, sensual, alluring, yet pure. The child cannot conceive the possibility that she must tolerate such sadistic abuse by the father during sex, the discovery of which poses a tremendous psychic burden when revealed. It is the most scandalising, heartbreaking, and supreme betrayal experienced when the child finds out that his mother makes love to his father rather than to himself.

If this internal conflict is left unresolved, the Madonna–Prostitute complex manifests, and women are split into Virgin-Mothers and Prostitutes. *The Empress* is thus the unsplit version of the oedipal mother, her unadulterated expression. She is the simultaneous embodiment of the two polarities, Mary and Venus. Yet still, both are mothers, one to Jesus and the other to Cupid, respectively.

The Queen of Swords, alternatively, is *the Castrating Mother*. The Castrating Mother is the term used to refer to the terrifying, persecutory, punishing version of the mother. Recall that the parents are seen by the child as omnipotent. Perspectives on God and a relationship to a divine parent are influenced by infantile perceptions of the power and authority held by the parents.

While religious sentiments are beneath the dominion of the superego, the child's superego is influenced more by the parents' own superego than by the parents themselves. It is the contents of the parental superegos that are emptied onto the child. During the phallic period, the superego makes its debut as part of the structural organisation of the mind.

If the Oedipus complex dissolves properly, the child, rather than viewing the father as a competitor, will view him as a model for himself. He will see his mother not as his wife but as a model for his future spouse, despite having special feelings for and from her. I will discuss this triangular relationship in a later chapter, but it was necessary to describe the proper dissolution of the Oedipus complex before discussing one of its pathological dissolutions.

I have exposited what happens when the masochistic feelings, perceived as deserved for the infringement of the incest taboo, are projected onto the figure of the father. He transforms into the figure of Laius, the *King of Swords* – the Castrating Father. Anxiety due to the severity of the superego floods the psyche of the child, and punishment arising from oedipal guilt is invested into him.

In an alternative dissolution, rather than the father being the executor of Oedipal punishment, it is the mother. This fear and dread are called 'castration anxiety'. It is called such because it is directed towards the organ that led the child to sin in the first instance.

As in the sin of Eve, she was not punished through her hands, which allegedly held the fruit. She was neither punished through her eyes, which saw the fruit, nor through her nose, which smelt the sweet scent of the fruit. Nor was she punished through her lips, which tasted the fruit. She was punished through the pain of childbirth. Recall that God is perfectly just; hence, the punishment always fits the crime. Why would the sexual and reproductive organ be subject to punishment if, allegedly, it did not participate in the sin?

Thus, castration anxiety, in truth, is simply anxiety regarding the organ that has caused him to infringe the incest taboo—the sin of sexual desire towards the beloved yet forbidden object. The child, in this instance, fears genital dismemberment for oedipal desire. In less severe and more symbolic instances, the child will feel, either presently or as an adult, a fear of being dominated, degraded, or made insignificant.

Paranoiac hallucinations in schizophrenia, for instance, may be tied to the persecutory feelings of the castration complex. Kitahara (1976) examined 111 societies, finding that circumcision was most common in societies where male children were likely to sleep with their mothers while their fathers resided in another dwelling place. The child is thus emasculated and made ineligible to copulate with the mother. He is retaliated against for desiring his mother and is punished accordingly.

Had he stolen, his hands would have been cut off. If he had looked at another man's wife, he would have been blinded. But because he desired his mother, the object that both incited his desire and with which he sought to fulfil it is mutilated, disfigured, and circumcised.

The mother who is not seductive but rather terrifying, and into whom all oedipal punishment is invested, is the *Queen of Swords*. The mother who was once nurturing is now persecutory. The figure of the terrifying (castrating) mother, like the terrifying father, is constructed from the material of the child's fears (Klein, 1953). If the mother is nagging, strict, frequently uses spanking, disputes with the father, or is unaffectionate, she can contribute to the image of the castrating mother.

The former infinite fount of love and tenderness disappears and is replaced by an omnipotent and condemning figure. Love is replaced by hate, safety is replaced by fear, and indulgence is replaced by cruelty. This is the *Queen of Swords*.

The *Queen of Swords*, as the name suggests, bears a sword. Her head is adorned with a crown of butterflies and a red veil. She is more austere and authoritative than her husband. She wears a cloak and cape that reflect the blue skies and white clouds. Her throne is the same as her husband's. Her domain is not over the earth but rather the sky above. Her facial expression, and the solitary bird above her, indicate sorrow, but also the wisdom and resilience born of that sorrow.

Analytically, the Queen of Swords represents the mother who enforces the law of incest prohibition with a cold, detached authority. The sword she wields is not merely a symbol of power but also of the psychological castration she enacts, eliminating the child's forbidden desires and executing him for his Oedipal love. Her crown of butterflies symbolises her psychic transformation, from the loving mother to the Castrating Mother. Her throne in the heavens, identical to the King of Swords', places her in a position of equal authority, ruling not over the earth but over the intellectual and moral realms, the domain of the superego. Her facial expression shows that she has left behind the warmth of maternal love and now wishes to kill her son.

In the case of the girl, the Queen of Swords is the mother as terrifying, powerful, and jealous. Dahl (1989) identified these qualities as synonymous with the witch-mother complex. The girl views the mother as retaliatory due to her secret erotic desire towards her father. This is created through the daughter's projection onto the mother of her own envious, hostile, and possessive aspects of her love. Clients who exhibit the witch-mother complex view their mothers as hostile and destructive towards their own interests, yet simultaneously powerful, awe-inspiring, and vivid, the figure of a persecutory queen. Dahl explicitly calls this "an Oedipal fantasy."

The Knight of Swords is the child as the Oedipal contestant. His sword is smaller compared to his father's (the King of Swords), and his stature and age, represented by the horse that pleads with the knight for gentility, set him up for failure. It should be noted that the Knight of Swords is supposed to be a prince in other tarot systems, so indeed this is the son of the king.

The only feminine depiction of a king is found in the King of Cups. This is the effeminate father who has lost his phallus to the child, hence the fish, slouching like a flaccid penis. The King of Cups is the father who has lost the Oedipal battle for the mother. Recall also that Water is a feminine element, as is Earth.

I have exposited plainly and considerably the triangulation of the King, Queen, and Knight of Swords. The Court of Swords represents the hostile aspect of the Oedipus complex.

$$King — Queen — Knight$$

Notice how the Queen acts as a buffer between the King and the Knight. She is also the love object and the object of competition for both the King and the Knight, hence her positioning in the Tarot.

Having sufficiently explained this, I shall now move on

to the dissolution of the Oedipus Complex as depicted in the Tarot.

The positive development of the superego is represented by the Hierophant. Religious and moral values, as represented by the Pope, are established, and the Ego and Id (the lily- and rose-vested priests) must obey. In this card, we see the Pope bearing the papal cross in his left hand. This is the same sceptre which, once vertical and bulbous, is now adorned with three vertical lines. As mentioned previously, Mendel (1949) interprets the horizontal line as feminine and the vertical line as masculine. The superego has come to an agreement with the inner masculine and feminine forces and oversees the activities of the Id (Rose Priest) and Ego (Lily Priest).

The negative development of the superego is represented by *the Hanged Man*, symbolising Oedipal failure (Rosengarten, 2000). The child is condemned to be castrated and hung like a flaccid, castrated penis. His shame is to be made known to the entire world, yet his illumination regarding the nature of sex and his own sexual nature is irrevocable. This illumination is represented by the halo around his head and his serene expression.

The Devil represents *Oedipal guilt* (Rosengarten, 2000). The sin of incest has been paid, and both participants in the *Oedipal fantasy* are punished. For this reason, the individuals in *The Lovers* card are the same as those in *The Devil* card. The Father has enchained the Mother for her infidelity and his Son for his betrayal. Adam and Eve are depicted animalistically because they have been reduced to their primal instincts. The woman's tail bears the fruit, the symbol of her role as *Temptress*. The *Devil* lights the boy's tail aflame, for it is his own primitive nature that has ignited his passions, and now he must be punished. The

Mother is not physically chastised, for her only crime was love. The Son is castigated for his love and lust.

In contrast, *Justice* is the positive resolution of the Oedipus Complex. The child has assimilated both Father (sword, penis) and Mother (scales, breasts) into himself as objects of power and fortification rather than passion and pain. *Justice* is a card of equilibrium, and the child has come to terms with his reality. The drape behind *Justice*, which conceals the inner temple, represents the infantile amnesia that occurs after the dissolution of the Oedipus Complex. In this depiction of *Justice*, she is not blind. Blindness represents *castration* (Dundes, 2009), and because the child has not been castrated, neither the Mother nor the Father is minacious. The sword is not threatening, rather, ostentatious.

King of Wands, quite simply, is the post-Oedipal father. He bears his penis proudly; yet, unlike the King of Swords, he is beneficent, pacific, and non-competitive. The Queen of Wands, alternatively, represents penis envy (Rosengarten, 2000).

As for the personage of the mother, she remains The Empress, for she has not been transformed as the father has, but rather given to the father (either at a loss or as a compromise).

LATENCY

Justice may also represent latency itself, for it implies the acceptance of the external world as an imposing force upon the ego. Because latency itself is not a libidinal stage, but rather a libidinal *dormition,* I do not find it best represented among any of the cards in the Major Arcana. Latency proper is best characterised as existing in the space between the structured psychic era of Justice and the continued rule of the superego (*Hierophant*). The card closest to representing latency, however, is The Sun.

The image of *The Sun* is one of confidence, warmth, and joy; but this joy is not the naïve joy of *The Fool*. It is a refined, sublimated joy, produced as the result of drives that have been successfully repressed and rerouted into acceptable and blameless forms of expression such as play and learning. The dynamism found in *The Sun* represents the redirection of energy towards school and play. This, precisely, is the psychological tone of latency.

The naked child riding a white horse in The Sun suggests a liberated ego that has emerged from the Oedipal conflict triumphantly. The child is no longer in a state of tension or confusion, nor is he ridden with guilt or anxiety. He has reintegrated the psychic energies that once revolved around Oedipal desire and now enjoys a harmonious self, basking in the light of the ego-ideal (a function of the superego) represented by the shining sun. His nudity indicates a lack of shame, the superego being supportive rather than punitive. The horse represents strength and sublimation: the ego has learnt to ride and harness the drives rather than be overpowered by them. He is still, nonetheless, a child and does not possess the maturity of *The Chariot* (more on this later).

This interpretation, however, remains unsatisfying. The Sun is best reserved for another representation, as shall be exposited later.

GENITALITY

The genital phase is characterised by mature sexuality, a disinclination towards the nuclear unit, and an inclination towards the achievement of sexual relationships. This phase begins at the onset of puberty, when hormonal and neurochemical shifts generate and stimulate sexual sensations and fantasies (Sisk & Zeher, 2005). The libido, after a period of dormancy (debatable), resurrects and is discharged onto healthy sexual objects. Rather than concentrate in the mouth, anus, or urethra as in previous times (Freud, 1905/1953), it is now concentrated in the genitals and their sensations.

Genitality, despite what is commonly proposed by critics, is not simply about the attainment of sex, but rather the attainment of intimacy most keenly manifest during the act of coitus. It is the achievement of a close and intimate relationship with another person. We require passion and emotion to live; thus, genitality is denoted by the ability to attain that very same passion and emotion through the experience of sexual and passionate love.

Hence, genitality is represented by the *Two of Cups*, also known as 'The Lord of Love'.

The *Two of Cups* shows a man and a woman joining hands in marriage. At the union of their hands emerges a caduceus. From the caduceus blossoms a chimera. Between them, in the foreground, stands a house on a hill.

This represents the maturation of the *sexual instinct*. The former idealistic and passionate fantasy of the *Oedipus complex* (*The Lovers*), with all its trials, tribulations, and dynamics, has now been *sublimated* and *dissolved* (Freud, 1924/1961) into a simpler form (*Two of Cups*). This is why *The Lovers* card has so many daunting elements: an archangel, Adam and Eve, a mountain, the *Tree of Life*, the *Tree of Knowledge*, and the serpent, whereas the *Two of Cups* is much more plain, depicting a woman with a laurel wreath, a man with a rose crown, two cups, a *caduceus*, a *chimera*, and a house on a hill.

The Lovers card is far more dense, heightened, and dynamic. The *Two of Cups* is comparatively bare, as are most of the *Minor Arcana*.

However, when we put these cards together, we can clearly see a connection. Those who may oppose my perspective of the book for being 'incoherent' will, in fact, see that it is quite coherent when the connections are made. Likewise, there are connections and references to the *Major Arcana* in the *Minor Arcana*, as in the case of *The High Priestess* and *The Two of Swords*.

Returning, when we put these cards side by side, we find the woman and the man in the *Two of Cups* in the same positions as *Adam and Eve* were: Adam and the man being on the right, with Eve and the woman on the left. In addition, you will find a hill between *Adam and Eve* as well as between the pair in the *Two of Cups*. In this situation, however, where there was once an *archangel*, now there is a *chimera*. Furthermore, both the *archangel* and the *chimera* possess the same wings. The *archangel* in *The Lovers* even has a *leonine* appearance.

Now that I have established the connection, allow me to enter upon an analysis.

This card represents, as mentioned, the mature sexual relations a child develops once he has grown out of childhood and reached maturity. This card is simpler than *The Lovers* because the *adolescent relationships* a child experiences do not equate with the *emotional intensity* of the *Oedipal drama*. Where there was once a grand mountain reaching heaven (creation, power, *infantile omnipotence*), now there is a home. The *mature sexual relationship* consists of *marriage*, a home, children, responsibilities, work, and the multitudinous concerns of a mature individual. The now mature child is no longer focused on the *romantic idealism* of the *Oedipus complex*, symbolised by the mountain reaching heaven. Rather, he is now focused on *earth*, *life*, and the laborious affairs of the *real world*.

The caduceus emerges from the hands of the couple. However, we see only the hand of the man in the centre, and not that of the woman. This is symbolic of marriage, for it is the boy who must grow into a man in order to one day propose to his wife. Seen in this way, we can perceive that, in this image, there is a proposal. This further illuminates the purpose of the caduceus and the chimera.

The caduceus emerges from the couple as a symbol of alchemical marriage. Psychoanalytically, this represents the sexual act and the consummation of marriage. The chimera, thus, is the offspring that is born out of marital intercourse. This child or chimera hangs over the couple and their home minaciously, for it threatens the former liberty the couple had as bachelors. It draws them in, and it consumes their whole life. More notably, however, it offers them a threat: the threat of Oedipal rivalry they themselves once exerted upon their own parents.

Is it any surprise, then, that their expressions are not joyful and content, or that the image of this card is not as merry as the Four of Wands? This card represents the disillusionment of romance and the responsibilities that come with mundane life, unlike that once lived in childhood. Indeed, the child has left the Garden of Eden (home) and now resides in nature (adult life). The comfort and relaxation of Eden have been abandoned, and the mature boy is now required to create his own home and provide for his family.

This card is called the Lord of Love. However, the Lord of Love is neither the woman nor the man, but the chimera. The child is the one who brings the woman and the man together. The chimera hovers over the home, and arguably the whole scene, representing not only the aforementioned ideas but also the potential conflicts that accompany parenthood. Yet, out of this, both people achieve the experience of love.

❧ 2 ❧
THE EGO, THE ID, & SUPEREGO IN TAROT

EGO

When describing the relationship between the ego and the id, Freud (1933/1961) refers to the ego as a horseman and the id as his horse. The horseman must tame the superior strength of the horse and guide it to where it needs to go. Yet, no matter how masterfully the horseman dominates his horse, he will never have complete and total control over it. He must do so by strength and authority, lest he lose control.

The ego, first and foremost, is connected to the body. It concerns itself with conscious awareness, perceptions, sensations, feelings, common sense, reason, and immediate memories. As mentioned in the introduction, the ego develops from the id, yet is not so sharply differentiated from it. The ego is the part of the id (passions and desires) that has been modified through the conditionings of the external world. The ego seeks pleasure, yet the principle of reality weighs against it, for not all pleasure is attainable.

Thus, the superego assumes its authority and adjudicates the ego, correcting and restraining it. The ego, therefore, is under constant supervision by the id, the superego, and the external world. Ironically, however, it believes itself to be master of all three.

For this reason, the ego is best represented in the Tarot by the card *The Chariot*. In this elegant image, we find the person of *The Fool*, having now gained mastery over the internal and external worlds. We see the Charioteer, crowned with a star, halo, sun, and laurel wreath. Above him is a canopy of stars. His shoulder plates are two-faced crescent moons. On his belt are astrological symbols, and on his skirt are symbols of alchemy. He too holds his own sceptre in his right hand.

Heralding the chariot are two sphinxes. An important, yet discreet, detail in this card lies in the reins of the sphinxes, or rather, their absence. The Charioteer does not control them by force but by telepathy. For this reason, although this card signifies personal mastery, success, and victory, it is also a card of false authority, undue confidence, and megalomania (Waite, 1911). Ouspensky (1913) states that it is quite possible that the smoke and fires of rebellion rise unknowingly in the city behind the Charioteer and warns that at any moment, if the Charioteer lose his concentration, he will lose the power of his magic word, and the sphinxes will turn around and devour him.

The representation of the ego as The Chariot should be quite obvious. *The Chariot* represents the ego as master of the body. *The Charioteer* is the child's ego, and the chariot itself is his body. The two sphinxes are the superego and the id. The city behind him is the external world, all of which he believes himself to be master of. It is worth emphasising that the person in The Chariot is the same as

The Fool, The Magician, and *The Hanged Man*. Likewise, he is the man in The Lovers card (the woman being his mate) and also *The Devil*. He may also be the man in the family depicted in the *Ten of Cups* and the *Five of Cups*, as well as the man depicted in the Two of Cups.

ID

The Id, as mentioned previously, is represented by The Magician. I shall avoid what I have elsewhere mentioned, and what I shall mention in sections to come, but I would like at present to note one detail especially. In this card, the setting of The Magician is heaven itself. There are no terreneal implications in the background of this card. Pamela Coleman Smith frequently drew the sky in gold, as seen in the Four of Wands and Ten of Swords. The roses and lilies, though meaningful, are merely symbolic ornaments. The Id is present from the beginning of conception; thus, the infinite environment that surrounds the magus represents the experience of pre-existence and primordiality in the womb. Before there was Ego, there was Id. We can imagine the expression of the Id in this state as saying, "I am God, and there is none other but I."

SUPEREGO

The Superego is not only a residue of the early object-choices of the Id and identifications, but also a reaction formation against those choices. By this latter statement, I mean the sexual feelings that arise towards both parents as a result of constitutional bisexuality. The Superego, under the influence of authority, religion, schooling, reading, and culture, will strengthen itself. As the child ages, he becomes gradually more exposed to each of these influences. As mentioned previously, the Superego is represented by *The Hierophant*. He is the esoteric Pope who teaches and interprets the mysteries. Psychoanalytically, he is the Superego endowed with all the powers of school, law, church, and culture.

3
THE INSTINCTS

Freud explored the role of the *Instincts* in *Instincts and Their Vicissitudes* (1915/1957), as well as *Beyond the Pleasure Principle* (1920/1955). He described the instincts as forces within the realm of the unconscious, at odds within the *Id*. These forces are divided in two: *Eros* and *Thanatos*. *Eros*, named after the God of Love, governs the sexual and survival instincts, as well as love. *Thanatos*, named after the God of Death, governs the sadistic instincts that compel the individual to destroy and return to the state of death, as well as hatred.

Eros and *Thanatos* are represented in the Tarot by *The Sun* and *Death* respectively, firstly by their mythological and archetypal resonance. *Eros* is the Roman equivalent of Cupid, frequently depicted as a child. In *The Sun*, we see a handsome boy-child riding a horse naked and wearing a red plume. This card represents the birth of life, or rather, new life. In *The Sun*, we see a naked boy, joyful, seated on a horse and holding a banner of victory. He is nude because he represents the infantile libido, free flowing and life giving, as *The Sun* itself nourishes the earth and makes it prosper with sunflowers.

In *Death*, we find *Thanatos* as the embodiment of death, perfectly typified. In the *Death* card, we see The Grim Reaper, or the fourth Horseman of the Apocalypse, Death himself. He has trampled over a king, while a woman laments and a child prays. He represents the termination, annihilation, and destruction of joy and life. He holds a flag with an inverted lily in the shape of the Goat-Star, for he is sadistic. For this reason, he symbolises the autonomous masochistic agent of the psyche that seeks to return oneself to pre-existence.

Upon closer look, one will sense that the two cards are connected. In the same way that *Eros* and *Thanatos* engage in a dynamic interplay, so too do the figures in *Death* and *The Sun*. Both are riding the white horse, and both are wearing the red plume. In *Death*, we even see the rising sun in the east.

It can be conjectured that the rider of the 13th Arcana is the little boy in the 19th. Both ride a horse and wear a plume. The rider of the pale white horse has died and been reborn. They are of the same substance, because Eros and Thanatos are of the same substance — the Id.

This is why we see the sun rising in the east in the drama of the *Death* card, because six scenes later he is reborn. It is a signal that the boy of *The Sun* card is to come. Hence why we must first pass through the pillars of *The Moon* card in the 18th Arcana (depicted in the east) in order to reach *The Sun*.

❧ 4 ☙
THE MAJOR ARCANA

Because the chapters that follow involve interpretations for each of the cards, I believe that this would be a prudent moment to discuss the dual aspect of the *Tarot*. It is true that there are cards that are more visually minacious than others (compare *The Sun* with *The Devil*), and some that are more emotionally charged (compare *Death* with *The Magician*). However, be this as it may, every card has a hidden warning. Every card within the *Major* and *Minor Arcana* has a positive and negative polarity, as well as a conscious and unconscious aspect. Every image has an appeal to *Thanatos* and an appeal to *Eros*, a light and a dark.

The 'negative' cards contain within themselves a hidden, refreshing message, and every inspiring message contains within itself a word of caution, perceivable only to the astute individual. The horror film *Tarot* (2024) may perfectly represent how the *Tarot* itself can not only introduce the illuminating insights of the repressed, but also the occulted, perverse, violent, and hidden. In *Jungian psychology*, this aspect of the self is referred to as the

Shadow. Freud regarded the *unconscious* as being ridden with these unacceptable, taboo, heinous emotions, thoughts, and fantasies.

In the film, *Tarot* characters come to life in grotesque and diabolical forms, targeting the weaknesses of each of the characters and forcing them to confront themselves. This film showed the characters achieving *anagnorisis*, especially with the unconscious (*shadow*) side of themselves, some failing and some triumphing. Hence, every *Tarot* image contains within itself hidden warnings and negative aspects, no matter how benevolent the image appears. *

Perhaps *The Sun* is the only card exempt from this. Many *Tarot* practitioners agree, though the negative interpretation of the card as representing naïveté or arrogance is certainly applicable.

A perfect example of this can be found in the *Five of Wands*, where consciously we perceive a celebration, but hidden in the crowd we find a person leering and jealous, consciously signifying the contempt that can arise in times of happiness, but unconsciously the *masochistic agent* (or *internal saboteur*) seeking our destruction. The *Minor Arcana* generally represent psychological particulars rather than fundamental forces of nature, life, philosophy, and the universe.

A challenger to my views might argue that they are interchangeable with the *Major Arcana*. However, with one comparison, one can easily see how the symbolism found in the Major Arcana is much more profound than the symbolism seen in the Minor Arcana. The Major Arcana, in my view, is more inquisitive, forcing the projector to ask himself what the symbol means and why such a card speaks to him in an almost imperceptible manner. In contrast, the Minor Arcana are more declarative and demonstrative of what the projector's inner world looks like. They very much represent worldly affairs, as Waite (1959) himself suggested. Though the Tarot itself reflects different themes of life, the Major Arcana is especially allotted this role.

Because of the profundity of the *Major Arcana*, it can easily perplex both practitioner and client. This is due to the activation of the *psychic filter*. When beholding a *Tarot* card, especially inquisitively, a communication occurs between the conscious and unconscious via the perception of the *Ego* (Freud, 1923/1961). Because the Major Arcana strongly appeal to the unconscious, consciousness is threatened by their depth and the internal significance is kept repressed. It is for this reason that individuals who study the Tarot at first are intimidated and almost stupefied by the profundity of the images. One knows that there is something deeper behind the cards, yet cannot accurately penetrate their meaning.

When the Major Arcana appear, it signifies several things about a client and the therapeutic process as a whole. Firstly, that the issue the client is dealing with is not a minor obstacle. It is neither a short inconvenience that shall soon pass nor a negligible event over the course of therapy. It is a major life event or a decisive therapeutic moment that requires intensive introspection. Whenever the Major Arcana appear, they urge the client to go within and reflect. The therapist would do well to dedicate several sessions to addressing the themes present in the card, and subsequently, the client's life.

When using the Tarot as a clinical tool, one is naturally faced with opposition and resistance. Any well-learned psychoanalyst will know that where there is resistance, there is change. When the Major Arcana appear clinically, they will tend to appear as *Guardians of the Threshold*, testing the client and therapist. The therapeutic practitioner must regard them as propellers forward.

Secondly, it may represent the client's stage in treatment or life, or the client themselves in relation to life and/or therapy. As mentioned, the *Major Arcana* represent significant themes and stages of life and personal growth. Thus, they express the nature of the external world, or the client in relation to the external world (i.e. *Ego-Mundus*). The therapist may, or may not, address how these themes or psychological states are affecting the client at this time.

Thirdly, the Major Arcana may represent powerful internal forces at work within the client's mind. As mentioned previously, they are the most symbolically profound images of the entire *Tarot*. When there are multiple *Major Arcanum* present, it means that the client is confronted with various *intrapsychic forces* or *internal objects*. This will often be the case with clients who are grievously overwhelmed.

It should be noted, however, that these interpretations are neither universal nor canonical and should be applied with discretion to every client. Different symbols mean different things to different persons. Yet a knowledge of the significance of the Major Arcana, and possible clinical interpretations, is essential to their productive usage. I have already explored the significance of several Arcana, but without further ado, I shall now delve into the clinical significations of the twenty-two *Major Arcana* of the *Tarot*.

0. THE FOOL

The Fool is inchoate, embryonic existence. The scene we behold takes place within the *mother's womb*. The client is confronting *pre-birth symbols*, inherited trauma, or *in utero*

events. The client, as the Fool, beholds the image of his pre-birth self: unformed, unshaped, and stepping blindly towards the fall of incarnation. Recall that *Rank*, in his *The Trauma of Birth* (1929/1993), linked the sensation the child feels when born with the sensation of falling. The precipice the Fool walks over is thus the *vaginal canal* through which the child 'falls' into birth.

On a more transcendental note, he is the unactualised version of the client, idealising and dreaming of the *Ego Ideal*. The Fool may also be represented as the *symbolic hero*, the *Tarot* being his journey.

Lastly, notice the *red plume* upon his cap. This is the same red plume present on *Death* and *The Sun*. The Fool is thus the uncreated potential of the client. He has not gone through collapse (*The Tower*), dissolution (*Death*), or rebirth (*The Sun*), but moves unknowingly towards these events as necessary outcomes in the process of personal growth and discovery. Bear in mind, however, that the Fool is number 0. He is neither beginning nor end, and may represent one or the other. If the client has experienced collapse, dissolution, and rebirth, the Fool may represent a new journey towards wholeness and awareness.

I. THE MAGICIAN

The *Magician* represents the *primary narcissism* of the infant. The *Ouroboros* around the waist of the Magician symbolises the self-centred perspective of himself in relation to the world around him. Accurately may it be said that his words and those of the infant child are the same: "All am I, and I am all."

When the Magician appears, it may well indicate that the client is in a state of activity or active embodiment of their ideals and drives. There is a channelling of *libidinal energy* directed towards a certain object or action.

The *wand* as a *phallic symbol* may also be considered, as well as other phallic imagery: the elongated cup, the sword, the staff, the snake itself. Hence, it may be said that the 'negative' polarity of the Magician in a clinical environment is *infantile narcissism*, trickery (of self or of therapist), and manipulation (the same applies).

II. THE HIGH PRIESTESS

The presence of the mother is undeniable in this image. This card, as in the case of *The Emperor*, *The Devil*, *The Fool*, *The Magician*, *The Empress*, and *The Hanged Man*, has been exposited previously. However, there are some aspects that have not been covered.

Notice the presence of water in this card, which seems to abound and overflow. The garment of *The High Priestess* blends with the water around her. As a matter of fact, the water itself appears to flow from her. This is the *amniotic water* of the womb. It may also represent *breast milk* (i.e. the waters of life).

When this appears for a client, it usually denotes the era of infancy. It may also represent a sense of *inner knowing*. It may also symbolise an approach towards the threshold of *unconsciousness*. This is because the High Priestess is the guardian of the *inner temple*; in order to access the garden and waters behind her, one must gain entry through her.

Inversely, this card may represent a personal sense of confusion or disorientation on the part of the client, possibly enmeshment or overwhelm. If female, it may also signify a confrontation with the *internal mother*. If male, it may represent the same, but also attachment to the pre-oedipal mother.

III. THE EMPRESS

I have elaborated much regarding *The Empress* in previous sections, therefore I shall not speak much. However, now would be a good moment to discuss the connection between *The Empress* and *The High Priestess*. The reason why these two cards are so intertwined is that they both represent the *mother*, but at different stages. As mentioned previously, the former is the *oedipal mother* and the latter the *pre-oedipal mother*. Water also runs in *The Emperor* as well, denoting the presence of the mother.

When the Empress appears clinically, it denotes the realm of oedipality and the oedipal mother. It may also represent generativity, creativity, and reproduction, since The Sun and Judgement are connected to this card. It may, of course, represent motherhood as a whole.

Alternatively, it may indicate dependency on the oedipal mother. It may denote a call for regression to an earlier stage. It may also represent a retention of libido rather than a prudent discharge.

IV. THE EMPEROR

THE EMPEROR.

Much has been exposited regarding this card for the reader to achieve a symbolic understanding; however, let it be known that this card represents the *essence of masculinity*. It is heavily *phallic*: the martial colours, the four heads of *Aries*, the crimson sky, the rugged mountains, the bearded man.

When this card manifests for a client, it represents the *masculine inverse* of *The Empress*. The client may be confronting the internal father. Alternatively, it may represent the tyrannical superego. Holistically, the client may be searching for stability, or attaining it.

V. THE HIEROPHANT

As elaborated previously, *The Hierophant* is a representative of the *superego*. Clinically, it may also represent the *sociological institution(s)* beneath which the client is subject. On a *negative polarity*, it may signify the *guilty conscience*. There may occur a dynamic in which the superego is the *pope* and the ego is *Martin Luther*. In this instance, the ego wishes to liberate itself from the tyranny and injustice of the superego and seeks to oppose it. Naturally, this may lead to the destruction of the superego and the *internal objects*; this, in turn, can lead to *suicide* (Friedman, 1967).

When this card appears clinically, as in the case of the cards which depict characters between two pillars, it may also represent that the client and therapist are approaching a certain threshold of *unconscious content*. However, whereas *The High Priestess* invites entry (so long as one is prepared to venture into the depths), *The Hierophant* excludes and keeps aback. The therapist must be *sagacious* in how he proceeds.

VI. THE LOVERS

This most beautiful card depicts the union of opposites. Intrapsychically, it represents the internal parental couple as a whole. On a positive note, it signifies harmony between the two internal parental objects. The negative represents the inverse: a split, separation, or disharmony. Psychosexually, it represents heterosexuality and homosexuality. In the therapeutic journey, it signals that the client approaches either a triumph or a fall. This card is also a depiction of constitutional bisexuality. Chiefly, however, it represents the Oedipus complex.

I would like to explore this card further in relation to the Oedipus complex. Despite its beauty and magnificence, we detect a particular kind of tension. No figure in this quaternity is mutually focused on another. The serpent whispers to Eve, Eve directs her attention to the archangel, the archangel to the scene below, and Adam adores Eve. Symbolically, this depicts the conflicted object choice the child faces and navigates during oedipality. The child must navigate taboo (serpent), desire (Eve), and morality (archangel).

As mentioned previously, the archangel overshadows the entire scene as the Law-giving father, who watches, judges, prohibits, and casts the child out of Eden. The light that shines above him is the superego. Though both parents contribute to the voice of the superego, the influence of the father is particularly potent.

VII. THE CHARIOT

Sequentially, this card announces that the union of opposites has been achieved, the internal parents are in accord, the Oedipus complex is resolved, and the ego emerges from the conflict as victor. He must, however, take care not to be too prideful, lest the conflict re-emerge, frictions arise, and he lose control of his sense of tranquillity. In other words, he must take care that the sphinxes of his mind serve him well and do not devour him.

The card is a depiction of masculine identification and the pursuit of power and autonomy. The Charioteer does not yet face castration anxiety (*Justice*, *The Hanged Man*, *The Devil*, etc.). Rather, he is embodying the grandiose ego ideal. The ego has aligned itself with the heroic paternal imago.

The card may also represent phallic narcissism. This is indicated by the upright position, the vertical design, the magic wand, and partially through the lingam-yoni.

VII. STRENGTH

Strength depicts the repression of the base instincts. She is an echo of Vulcanus Stata Mater, the fire goddess who held back the wrath of Vulcan and prevented destruction.

Psychologically, Stata Mater represents the feminine force that contains the wild masculine force.

Interestingly, the Lion is a symbol of fire, hence it is the image of Leo. Leo is also a masculine sign according to the Ptolemaic system, which identifies masculine and feminine signs based on alternating sequences beginning with the masculine Aries and ending with the feminine Pisces. It is also considered masculine by the hemispheric system of Firmicus Maternus, who attributes the signs in the hemisphere of Cancer a nocturnal nature, and thus feminine, and inversely those in the hemisphere of Leo a diurnal nature, and thus masculine.

The eruption of the volcano psychologically represents the eruption of the unconscious and its catastrophic (or transformative) effects upon consciousness. In depictions of the Virgin Mary as advocate, we see her bearing her breast to a wrathful Jesus and holding back the vengeful arm of her son, most often wielding a thunderbolt and prepared to strike the earth.

Joseph is depicted in *The Annunciation* by St. Romanos as crying out in reverential fear before Mary, saying: "O shining one, I see a flame and glowing brightness around you; and so, Mary, I am struck with amazement. Protect me and do not consume me! Your chaste womb has suddenly become a furnace full of fire; then do not, I beg of you, melt me, but spare me. You wish that I, too, like Moses long ago, take off my sandals and draw near you."

Strength is the image of the mother who tempers the wild passions of the masculine psyche, or Eros. The bridle at her waist with which she harnesses the lion represents chastity. Clinically, she is also a defence against chaos and trauma. She does not tame the lion by force, for the lion is certainly stronger than she; nor does she tame the lion by hypnosis, for her eyes are closed, though he stares into hers. She tames the lion by wisdom, as indicated by the infinity symbol above her head, a sign of the magician's hat.

Fire is desire, aggression, sexuality (as opposed to sensuality), and masculinity. Note that she does not destroy the lion but tames it. The libido is contained so as not to cause a collapse of the psyche. She ensures that the city of the mind is not consumed by the magma of the unconscious, for she tempers the destructive impulses. In a way, she is the maternal superego. In a negative polarity, this can become castrating. The id shall break through the superego unless Strength intervenes.

IX. THE HERMIT

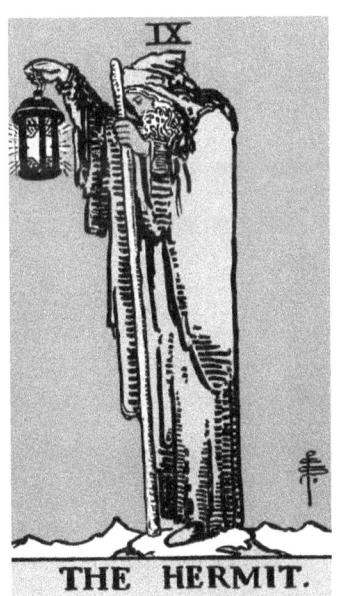

The Hermit is a symbol of turning inward, disconnection, and introspection. The client has begun the process of turning away and individuation, either from primary objects or from the therapist himself. The star he holds in the lantern indicates that they have oriented their thoughts more towards purpose and philosophy, namely existentialism.

When this card appears in the clinical journey, it may indicate that the harsh superego has been transformed into an inner guide. It is now more aligned with the ego than in previous times. The client may begin to withdraw from therapy and experiment with greater autonomy. In therapy, the client may also begin to employ regression, not as a defence, but in order to revisit the past and reorganise.

On the negative polarity, this card may indicate depression, the depressive position, or that the client is going through the dark night of the soul. Alternatively, the libido may be withdrawn and the ego may exist in a more isolated state. The client is not acting out their instinctual drives. The goal should be to transform this act into sublimation and direct the libido towards more intellectual, artistic, or philosophical pursuits. It must be ensured that the client has not withdrawn completely from pleasure by transforming the action of the ego into contemplation and learning.

X. WHEEL OF FORTUNE

The phenomenon of repetition compulsion is best represented by the Wheel of Fortune. One rises and falls according to the compulsions of the unconscious. This card is ultimately a symbol of progression. *Christian Meditations on the Tarot* (1980/1985) assigns the following excerpt from the Nicene Creed to this card:

"For us men and for our salvation he came down from heaven: by the power of the Holy Spirit he became incarnate from the Virgin Mary, and was made man... he ascended into heaven and is seated at the right hand of the Father."

The serpent (Typhon) on the left represents the instinctual drives and the libido in its primal form. It may also symbolise Thanatos moving downward to a state of death, destruction, and dissolution. Anubis below represents the ego rising. He signifies the developing ego, capable of sublimation and mediating between the instinctual and moral demands. Naturally, the sphinx above represents the ego as master. The individual has attained self-mastery and has integrated all the skills necessary to employ healthy psychic manoeuvres.

This position is not stable, however. Mastery must be re-learned and practised continually. The return of the repressed is always possible. In this card, we see the (psychic) evolution from serpent to sphinx.

Directing our attention to the four apocalyptic beasts from Ezekiel's vision that adorn the corners of the image, we see the angel (Aquarius), eagle (Scorpio), bull (Taurus), and lion (Leo), all reading books. The angel represents the ego in its most intellectual and sagacious form. The eagle is the symbol of transformed drives, sublimated in their highest and most prudent form. The bull is present to control and mediate the psyche. The lion embodies the narcissistic libido, channelised into self-assertion and pride. Together, these denote the four corners of the structured self and the psychic faculties required to maintain inner stability.

On a clinical level, the client may be confronting the past or evolving. It would be interesting to explore which characters they are naturally drawn to or identify with, in order to clarify therapeutic focuses. On a negative note, the card may also represent a lack of control, both inner and outer.

XI. JUSTICE

Justice is the manifestation of the superego in its structural and developed form. I have discussed this card previously as well; namely, it is the superego formed from the oedipal resolution. As mentioned before, the characters in the Tarot that stand between two pillars and before a veil indicate the psychic structures that exist at the thresholds of the mind. The superego stands at the gateposts of the unconscious, guarding both that which is assimilated and that which is actuated. The figure is androgynous because it is neither father nor mother; rather, it represents what they both become within. The individual is no longer governed by love or hate, but by duty.

This card may denote either moral anxiety or castration anxiety, depending on whether it is positively or negatively represented. I have discussed this previously, too.

XII. THE HANGED MAN

Waite, in his *Pictorial Key*, considers this the most central of all the cards in the Tarot, perhaps because it relates directly to the Oedipus complex. We see the Hanged Man suspended by the foot, alive yet immobilised and serene. This represents the client who has not renounced the oedipal object (usually the mother), lost at the hands of the oedipal and castrating father, and who cannot identify with the father or his laws. He is thus a fugitive, condemned for his opposition to the paternal prohibition of the mother. He is an oedipal failure. Justice has deemed him guilty of incest and has sentenced him to castration. His halo represents his awareness of sexuality, corroborated by its position at the bottom of the card (i.e. the genital area). The therapeutic and clinical implications are clear.

XIII. DEATH

I would like to say, first and foremost, that this card is not a card of mortal death. Rather, it is a card of endings and new beginnings. Death does not hold a scythe, but a flag. He has not come to kill, but to announce. This is therefore a representation of symbolic death as an essential aspect of development. Sequentially, the old order of oedipality (represented by the clerical and monarchical figures) is passing away, and the new order of incestuous renunciation (the Lutheran flag and rising sun in the east) approaches. It is the death of the incestuous wish, the renunciation of the primary object, and the acceptance of taboo. The infantile ego, represented by the child at the horse's feet, must now fall. The loss of innocence has not transpired in a romantic fashion.

Clinically, it is time for the client to release the past and undergo a symbolic death, no matter how painful it may be, in order to catalyse rebirth. This is not a death of destruction, but of resurrection. As mentioned previously, this card also represents Thanatos.

XIV. TEMPERANCE

Quite simply, in *Temperance*, the ego has begun to reform. After the death of the Oedipal fantasy, the ego must restructure itself. The drive and raw instinct have now been transformed and redirected towards more prudent pursuits such as art, ethics, and love. The subject has begun to balance the demands of Eros and Thanatos. Of course, the psyche is naturally in a state of constant flux, and thus we cannot discern whether the water is moving upwards or downwards. The archangel depicted is not punitive or judgemental, but balanced, harmonious, and concise. It is the ego, now reconciled with the id and superego. He has one foot in the unconscious (water) and one foot in the conscious (land). This is not a state of fragmentation or splitting, but of stability. The triangle contained within the square alludes to the number three (as mentioned previously), but also to the Id, Ego, and Superego contained within the order of the mind. The path from the pond to the sun represents the journey from repression to sublimation. The solar crown does not imply narcissistic grandiosity, but illumination and personal revelation.

Therapeutically, this may indicate the respective restructuring phase in which the client, now imbued with the wisdom of therapy, can begin to assimilate the previous clarity into himself and strengthen the ego. This is a card of balance and harmony.

XV. THE DEVIL

As mentioned before, The Devil represents Oedipal guilt. Here we see an image heavily saturated with shame, fixation, instinctual bondage, and the failure of sublimation that had been momentarily achieved in Temperance.

Why does the aversive image of The Devil come after the illuminating image of Temperance? In The Devil, we see the return of the repressed. None of the traumas, forbidden wishes, or repressed contents ever truly disappear. One either makes peace with them or does not. The Devil marks the moment these repressed contents return in a more destructive form. The erupted repressed material was too shameful and too incestuous to be resolved.

What is initially striking is that we once again find the figures of The Lovers, but now in an infernal setting, in contrast to the former paradisiacal one. This is the Oedipal complex now debased, degenerated, and stripped of all former romance and intense affect. It is no longer idealistic, but perverted. In The Lovers, we see an archangel towering above the couple, representing the watchful, paternal superego. Now, the paternal superego has become horrifying, omnipotent, and persecutory. His left hand burns the tail of the son in punishment for his crime. If we accept the tail as a phallic symbol, we can interpret this action as one of castration. The superego no longer guides, but torments.

The inverted pentagram, or the Goat-Star, represents matter over spirit. It also signifies the triumph of the inferior world over the superior world, the world of light overcome by the world of darkness. Psychoanalytically, this represents the triumph of the unconscious over the ego. We see the right hand of the Devil marked with the symbol of black magic, the sign of Saturn. Psychoanalytically, this may symbolise the mark of shame that accompanies masturbation, that is, masturbatory guilt.

In actuality, The Devil is also a threshold figure, not because he stands between two pillars, but because he is the pillar itself. His two pillars are Adam and Eve, now debased and enchained. Their nudity is no longer pure, heavenly, or sublime; it is shamed and displayed. These are the shadows and remembrances of the Oedipus complex. In therapy, one must pass through The Devil as a final ordeal.

XVI. THE TOWER

In this card, we see the literal demolition of the Oedipus complex (Freud 1924/1961). The lightning falling from heaven, representing either God or nature, symbolises the principle of reality and morality destroying the false and the fantastical. The child realises that he is not the centre of the universe, and his sense of importance and narcissism has been severely injured. He is dealt a narcissistic blow through the realisation that his parents are not perfect—or worse, that they do not love him unconditionally.

The upheaval we witness in The Tower represents the collapse of the superego. The lightning striking The Tower also signifies the unbearable truth that has shattered fantasy. The tower itself is the fortress of the ego. This fortress, however, is built on falsehood and evasive defences rather than healthy strength. For this reason, other names for this card include *The Tower of Babel* and *The Tower of Destruction*. It is not called *The Tower of Light* or *The Tower of Safety*. The crown that falls from the top of the tower signifies the loss of the superego's authority. The superego has failed and is now in crisis.

In therapy, this card may denote breakthrough sessions and emotional catharsis. With my clients, I have also, on numerous occasions, witnessed this card emerge when a client has built and invested time and energy in a lie. This individual must now start from scratch, but for the better. No matter how painful this change may be, it is always for the better, as I have mentioned. The therapist must help the client confront the sense of guilt and helplessness, but more importantly, face the truth.

XVII. THE STAR

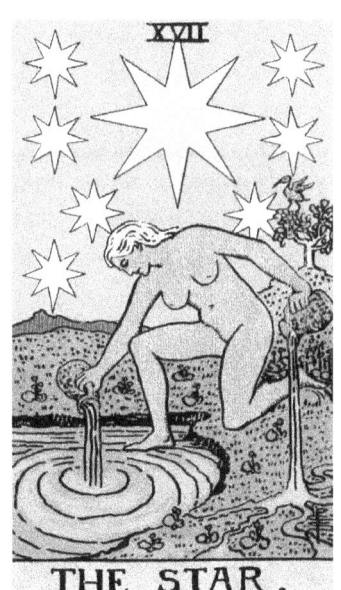

The Star represents the psychic reparation that follows the catastrophes of The Tower and The Devil. It is also associated with the oceanic feeling described by Freud in

(1930/1961), symbolised by her foot in the pond. The oceanic feeling is the term used to describe a sense of oneness with the universe and creation itself, a sense of purpose.

In this card, we see a naked woman feeding both a pond and the land with water from her two pitchers. Nudity here signifies vulnerability and the stripping away of ego defences following their collapse in The Tower. The woman represents the ego in a state of openness. She has returned to a primal state, not through defensive regression, but in a restorative way. She is restoring the unconscious, symbolised by the pond, as well as the conscious mind, symbolised by the land.

The superego is seen here as the golden star (Sirius) shining amidst the seven pale stars (the seven classical planets). In its current form, it is no longer prohibitory or persecutory; it is now the guiding ideal. The ibis of Thoth, perched upon the tree, symbolises wisdom. The client has now directed their attention towards the process of self-discovery and healing. They have attained all the required psychic tools and experience needed to proceed successfully. The ibis therefore signals a movement from trauma towards meaning.

This card has appeared to me in cases where clients, mostly women, are focused on re-learning self-love.

XVIII. THE MOON

In *The Moon*, we remain in the same environment as *The Star*, except our perspective has shifted. In fact, we are now in the foreground of *Death*, and rightfully so. *The Moon* is a naturally ominous card, and the emotions it exudes are markedly different from those of *The Star* and *The Sun*.

Ouspensky (1913) describes the scene as follows:

"A desolate plain stretched before me. A full moon looked down as if in contemplative hesitation. Under her wavering light, the shadows lived their own peculiar life. On the horizon, I saw blue hills, and over them wound a path which stretched between two grey towers, far away into the distance. On either side of the path, a wolf and a dog sat and howled at the moon. I remembered that dogs believe in thieves and ghosts. A large black crab crawled out of the rivulet into the sands. A heavy, cold dew was falling. Dread fell upon me. I sensed the presence of a mysterious world, a world of hostile spirits, of corpses rising from graves, of wailing ghosts. In this pale moonlight, I seemed to feel the presence of apparitions; someone watched me from behind the towers, and I knew it was dangerous to look back."

Ouspensky thus introduces us to the scene of *The Moon* by first taking us into a 'desolate plain'. This plain represents the psychic blankness during analysis that invites projection, fantasy, and anxiety to take form. This emptiness does not comfort; rather, it overwhelms with dread because the ego cannot anchor itself. The moon is not a guide, but a witness. Thus, her 'contemplative hesitation' reflects the angst of consciousness when confronted with the emergence of the unconscious, for not everything hidden desires to be made known. The living shadows described by Ouspensky recall Freud's notion of *The Uncanny* as that which is both familiar and foreign, and therefore feared.

The setting of *The Moon* lies within the domain of the unconscious id, where dreams, phantasms, and archaic remnants reign. Alternatively, the moon in this image is not the nurturing mother of *The Empress*; rather, she is the inconceivable and powerful archaic, primitive mother figure. From here emerge the anxiety dreams and infantile fears of being chased and consumed, rooted in our primitive history. Hence, the towers signal the threshold of the primitive mind and the entrance into primal anxiety.

The dog, a domesticated and civilised animal, represents the ego. The wolf, wild and untamed, represents the id. Both howl at the moon, signifying the disturbance each psychic structure experiences when stirred by the primitive mind. The crab emerging from the water symbolises the surfacing of primal, infantile fears from the depths of the unconscious.

His vision of the dog and the wolf is perhaps the most striking of the entire vision, especially in their relation to "thieves and ghosts". This phrase is steeped in projection and displacement. The dog (ego) is alerted not because it knows what is in the unconscious, but because it senses what has been repressed. This is elaborated on further when he describes the setting of *The Moon* as *"a mysterious world, a world of hostile spirits, of corpses rising from graves, of wailing ghosts."* These corpses, ghosts, and spirits are the childhood memories, sexual fantasies, forbidden wishes, and primal scenes of pre-infantile amnesia. The dreadful spirits present invisibly in this image may also represent entities of persecutory anxiety. Dundes (2009) mentions that the fear of ghosts and the practice of their appeasement are associated with guilt following the death of a loved one, that they may return to retaliate against the conscious or unconscious hateful wishes directed towards them. This "mysterious world" of *The Moon* is therefore full of internal persecutors and dead identifications.

His final statement, expressing fear to look back, is also deeply meaningful. It recalls the mythology of Eve and

Orpheus, whose act of "looking back" carried repercussions. The fear of looking back is resistance, the psychic force that prevents repressed content from becoming conscious. The ego knows that to see the contents of the unconscious fully would be disturbing. Interestingly, when Ouspensky refers to "looking back", he does not refer to the scene before him, but rather to the scene behind him. This insinuates the past, the primitive and ancient. Thus, the realm behind the card is both the ontogenetic and the phylogenetic past. To look back is to encounter the primal scene: the child's unconscious or partially conscious trauma of witnessing parental intercourse. This moment is simultaneously traumatic and erotic for the child, and is therefore the source of intense libidinal excitation.

The phrase *"someone watched me from behind the towers"* strongly evokes the conscience as a judgmental and guilty force. Looking back risks revealing not only the contents of the id, but also incurring guilt for having desired to look. The terror lies not merely in what one might see behind, *but in being caught wanting to see.*

Rightfully, *The Moon* is another threshold card. *The Moon* evokes the pre-verbal, prehistoric, evolutionary, tribal, and mythic past. To further corroborate the symbolism of the past in this card, the crab, the central figure of the image, walks backwards. When this card emerges in therapy, it may represent signal anxiety, but it may also indicate the need for Dream Work, Fantasy, Imaginal Work, or even Hypnosis.

XIX. THE SUN

In this most pleasant image, we see a handsome boy riding freely upon a white horse, holding a red banner and crowned with sunflowers. The sun shines brilliantly above him. In *The Sun*, we see the client who has made peace with the unconscious, his past, his traumas, and so forth, and is free from shame, guilt, and denial. The client now rides upon the drives, rather than allowing the drives to control him as in *The Chariot*. The sun itself is the good internal object, the kind, nurturing, and healing parent. The face of the sun is not grave as in *The Moon*; rather, it is mild and fair.

Sequentially, this card denotes the triumph over Death, darkness (*The Moon*), destruction (*The Tower*), and despair (*The Devil*). This card declares the victory of the life instinct. Vitality, libido, and life-affirming energy have broken through and now begin to animate. The naked boy is the embodiment of Eros. He is unashamed and joyous, riding openly in a state of pure libidinal delight. His arms are outstretched in erotic receptivity, free from guilt and punishment. He is unburdened by castration anxiety and the paranoia of the incest taboo. The bulbous sunflowers behind him, symbolic of solar worship, represent phallic and genital maturity as well as fertility. Ouspensky (1913) also recognises the reproductive symbolism of the card. The sun may also symbolise the benevolent superego.

When this card appears in therapy, it represents: ego synthesis; successful resolution of transference; freedom from pathological repression; acceptance of instinctual life; and affirmation of self and reality.

XX. JUDGEMENT

Judgement is rather interesting, as it is not interpreted simply. In the image, we see the Archangel Gabriel sounding the trumpet of resurrection and calling the souls of the prayerful dead in their coffins up to the heavens to be admitted to eternal life. On one level, we may interpret this clinically as representing the emergence of the repressed, not as something horrifying as in *The Devil*, but rather as a product of the therapeutic process, surrendering itself for judgement. Trauma, remembrances, complexes, and so forth now emerge from their coffins for their final resolution. Freud (1914) explained that when pathological psychic contents remain unresolved, the subject repeats them compulsively rather than remembering and letting go. *Judgement* marks the end of that repetition, the moment when the analysand recognises the repetition for what it is, and a symbolic death, resurrection, and transformation occur. Ouspensky senses this death and rebirth motif when he says, regarding his vision of the card, "I understood the meaning of birth in death." What has been buried and repressed is not only uncovered but also transformed.

On another level, one quickly notices the family constellation depicted. In fact, we see two families. Here we find the psychic family, now resurrected and consciously faced. This evokes the therapeutic resolution of the Oedipus complex. The oedipal situation has been brought up for therapeutic judgement. In this card, we witness two sets of three. Not only is the number three significant, as mentioned previously, but the number seven (the six mortals plus one archangel) also denotes psychic completion. In other words, it signifies the completion of the therapeutic work and the achievement of integration.

XXI. THE WORLD

At last, ego integration, fulfilment, and complex resolution have been achieved. *The World* denotes the sense of internal harmony, purpose, and transcendent wisdom experienced by the client when therapy is completed. This is a card of healthy secondary narcissism. The libido invests in the ego, but not in a grandiose way; rather, in a self-loving way. The ego ideal has been reabsorbed, and successful sublimation has been achieved.

This card is, more appropriately, a post-analysis image of the client. Suffering has been transformed into meaning, and disharmony has been conquered by harmony.

Ouspensky writes of this image: *"This is a vision of the world in the circle of Time, amidst the four principles. But thou seest differently because thou seest the world outside thyself. Learn to see it in thyself and thou wilt understand the infinite essence, hidden in all illusory forms."* The circle that encompasses the woman is not one of enclosure, but of plenitude.

❧ 5 ❧
THE MINOR ARCANA

As we have seen, the *Major Arcana* represent the primary complexes, psychic forces, and existential events that shape the architecture of the psyche. They also represent profound psychological experiences such as individuation, anxiety, and trauma. They touch the universal, the structural, and the all-encompassing.

The *Minor Arcana*, to which we shall now direct our attention, are not so universal or oceanic in meaning. They almost always manifest in a specialised way for each individual. Thus, the therapist must supplement their clinical knowledge of the client in the larger part of interpretation. Put simply, the *Minor Arcana* symbolise more particular expressions of psychic life. This may manifest as smaller dramas, minor complexities, or momentary strifes. In a more divinatory expression, they are the lived consequences of the major forces of life. These cards often depict neurotic fixations and perversions, imbalances of libido or psychic energy, subcomplexes (for example, inferiority, Cain, or Napoleon), or achievements and compensations.

The *Minor Arcana* are not as mythically structured as the *Major Arcana*. They represent the mundane and the daily vicissitudes of life. These are the neurotic entanglements, everyday defences, and emotional fluctuations of the personality that characterise the human condition. However, one must not confuse the *mundane* with the *insignificant*. There are certain moments within the so-called "ordinary" that bear disproportionate psychic weight, *nodal points* of development, if you will.

Hence, the *Two of Cups* or the *Queen of Swords*, though part of the *Minor Arcana*, are developmentally significant. *Not all minor events are minor in meaning.* Certain "minor" happenings of childhood bear lifelong weight, as any analyst knows.

In the following segments, I shall exposit each suit of the arcana, their significance, and each card within that respective suit. I will then conclude with an analysis of the court cards belonging to that suit. Before I begin, I must first exposit the significance of the structure of the four suits, the pip cards, and the court cards themselves.

THE FOUR SUITS

The number four is incredibly significant in philosophy, mythology, and psychology. Similar to the number three, the number four is also deeply present in our world schema. There are: Four Rivers of Eden – Pishon, Gihon, Tigris, and Euphrates; Four Angelic Princes of the Earth – Michael, Gabriel, Raphael, and Uriel; Four Ages of Man – Gold, Silver, Bronze, and Iron; Four Winds – Boreas, Notus, Eurus, and Zephyrus; Four Cardinal Virtues – Wisdom, Courage, Justice, and Temperance; Four Elements – Earth, Air, Fire, and Water; Four Evangelists and Gospels – St Matthew, St Mark, St Luke, and St John; the four points of the cross; the four-letter name of God; Four Directions – North, South, East, and West; Four Seasons – Spring, Summer, Autumn, and Winter; Four Lunar Phases – New, Waxing, Full, and Waning; Four Chambers of the Heart – Left and Right Atrium, Left and Right Ventricle; and Four Extremities of the Body – two arms and two legs.

Since 400 BC, the personality of individuals has been divided into four. Around this time, Hippocrates elaborated the theory of the four humours: blood, yellow bile, black bile, and phlegm. The characteristics associated with these humours were amorousness, irritability, despondence, and unemotionality, respectively. Aristotle, in the next century, expounded the four sources of happiness: *Hedone*, *Ethikos*, *Propraitari*, and *Dialogike*. Galen, in 190 AD, established the fundamental four temperaments: sanguine (liver), choleric (gallbladder), melancholic (spleen), and phlegmatic (lungs). Paracelsus proposed the four elemental spirits: Sylphs, Salamanders, Gnomes, and Undines, each with their own characteristics and all influencing human motives.

The twentieth century, of course, erupted with personality models, many of which employed a quaternary structure. Kretchmer (1921/1925) forwarded the Hypomanic, Hyperaesthetic, Depressive, and Anaesthetic types. Keirsey & Bates (1984) established the Dionysian, Apollonian, Epimethian, and Promethean personalities. Freud in 1931 proposed his libidinal types: Erotic, Narcissistic, Obsessional, and Blended. The psychosexual model itself is divided into four libidinal parts, and any individual may manifest characteristics of these respective stages: Oral, Anal, Phallic, and Genital.

1.0 The Four Divisions of Personality

Humour	Blood	Yellow Bile	Black Bile	Mucous
Season	Spring	Summer	Fall	Winter
Element	Air	Fire	Earth	Water
Organ	Liver	Gallbladder	Spleen	Lungs
Temperament	Sanguine	Choleric	Melancholic	Phlegmatic
Elemental Spirit	Sylphs	Salamanders	Gnomes	Undines
Character Style (Kretchmer, 1921/1925)	Hypomanic	Hyperaesthetic	Depressive	Anesthetic
Temperament (Bates, 1984)	Dionysian	Apollonian	Epimethain	Promethean
Characteristic	Amorous	Irascible	Despondent	Unemotional
Libidinal Type (Freud, 1931)	Erotic	Narcissistic	Obsessional	Blended
Erogenous Zone	Genital	Phallic	Anal	Oral

While the *Minor Arcana* generally illustrate the field of mundane life, including daily conflicts, character traits, and interpersonal events, on a deeper axis each suit corresponds with the erogenous zones in which the libido is focused, fixated, or expressed.

Firstly, the suit of *Cups* corresponds to the oral type. This suit reflects themes centred on dependency, longing, and emotionality. In the images of the cups, we see the libido expressed through attachment, emotional nourishment, or its absence. When fixated, this may produce clinging, melancholia, or affective dysregulation. When sublimated, it produces poetic sensitivity, reflectiveness, empathy, and emotional attunement. The *Cups* type is governed by a craving for intimacy and love, often repeating early maternal oral experiences. When stagnated, we may witness the opposite: lackadaisicalness, apathy, and disconnection. The latter is best reflected in the Four and Five of Cups. The *Cups*, in general, reflect the libidinal ache of love, connection, and loss.

The suit of *Pentacles*, very appropriately, corresponds to the anal libido. The images in this suit are predominantly concerned with money. Freud himself acknowledged the connection between the anal phase and money, symbolically associating the latter with faeces (1959). Anal characters are concerned with possession, control, withholding, and material fixation. During this phase, the child discovers autonomy, as well as control and manipulation of the environment, through the retaining or expulsion of faeces. The act of retaining and releasing also affords the child great pleasure. *Pentacles* reflect concerns over resources, cleanliness, order, and security. The Four of Pentacles depicts hoarding, while the Six may reflect the child's fantasy of giving gifts (that is, faeces) to the parent.

The suit of *Wands* corresponds to the libido in the phallic stage, bold, expressive, ambitious, and driven by assertion and visibility. The wands themselves are phallic symbols. The grass growing upon them may be a symbolic parallel to pubic hair. This phallic libido, as represented in this suit, concerns itself with action, power, and conquest. The images often reflect the sublimation of libido into achievement, attainment, and creativity, but may also depict narcissism, narcissistic injury (Ten of Wands), exhibitionism, oedipal rivalry (Five of Wands), or manic defences (Nine of Wands). The *Wands* reflect a need *to be seen* and *admired*. It is a performative and passionate investment of the ego ideal.

The suit of *Swords* reflects the libido concentrated in the genital zone. The *Swords* suit aligns with the genital stage, the stage of psychosexual and developmental maturity. Here, we find that the libido has been disciplined by the formation of the superego. Sometimes this discipline is tempered, while at other times it is harsh. At best, we see the ego governed by law, consequence, and order. Inversely, we also see shame, intellectualised defences, and cruelty. The libido may be expressed through discipline and discernment, or through self-lacerating guilt. More often than not, the *Swords* express the painful aftermath of moral structuring.

In this suit, we find themes of castration anxiety, harsh judgment, and inner conflict. In the imagery, we witness either a rise or a fall brought about by the process of maturation. This may also explain why the suit is characterised by rather bleak and severe depictions. The images are painful because they concern themselves with a confrontation with reality. It is important to note that the genital phase is not paradisiacal. The genital stage concerns itself with the awareness of loss, betrayal, infidelity, early trauma, sacrifice, and the resurgence of the repressed, all reflected in this suit. The question lies in whether one is capable of attaining mastery over one's inner conflicts.

Freud's 1931 typology proposes that libido can become characterologically organised in different ways, yielding three fundamental types: the erotic, the narcissistic, and the obsessional, followed by a blended type. Each type reflects a different dominant axis of libidinal investment, whether in others, in the self, or in ideals. Fromm (1947/1990), Porter (1976), and Maccoby (2002) elaborated on Freud's libidinal types by considering the social world, interpersonal motivation, sociology, and conflict as factors in libidinal development. By viewing the suits as symbolic mirrors of these libidinal types, we can enrich our understanding of the *Minor Arcana* not merely as events, but as psychic expressions of personality structure.

2.0 Libidinal Correspondences to the Suits

Suit	Libidinal Type	Libidinal Vector	Core Need	Psychic Structure	Fromm (1947/1990)	Cards	Aspect
Cups	Erotic / Caring	Others	Love	Id	Receptive	Two, Five	Tenderness, Longing, Heartbreak
Swords	Obsessive	Morality	Moral Certainty	Superego	Hoarding	Eight, Nine	Conscience
Wands	Narcissistic	Ego-Ideal, Self-Preservation	Admiration	Ego	Exploitative	Two, King	Ego-Expression
Pentacles	Erotic - Obsessive - Narcissistic (Blended)	External World	Security	Blended	Marketing	Four, Six,	Stability, Fear of loss.

The suit of *Cups*, as will become apparent, reflects the erotic or caring type. The images of the *Cups* pertain to emotional investment, love, and affection. In the *Two of Cups*, for instance, we see an image of emotional reciprocity. Fromm classifies this characteristic constellation as the *Receptive Orientation*, and Maccoby interprets it as the *Caring Type*. The *Two of Cups* shows the bliss of mutual attachment. The *Five of Cups*, alternatively, demonstrates the sorrow of its loss.

These personalities seek to merge with the other, to be held, to be loved, and to love in return.

The suit of *Swords* corresponds with the obsessional type. Here, the libidinal vector is no longer directed toward love or pleasure, but toward the superego, toward the psychic tribunal of moral certainty and conscience. This type is governed by an internal world of judgement, scrutiny, and self-restraint. In some cases, this can be rightful and even necessary. In others, however, it is self-punishing. The core need of this type is to be righteous, disciplined, and autonomous, yet beneath this need lies a gripping anxiety. The individual is superego-dominated. They submit to rules and guilt, their only safety being the clarity of conscience. The *Nine of Swords* speaks to the condemnation of internal adjudication, while the *Ten of Swords* is plagued by guilt and dread. *Swords* are instruments not only for defence, but also for self-torment.

In contrast, the Suit of Wands represents the narcissistic type. The narcissistic libido is manifest here, as well as the ego ideal and the preservation of self. The central need of the narcissistic type is recognition, power, and sexual admiration. The narcissistic structure is dominated by the ego and is less plagued by inner conflict. These individuals assert themselves into the world rather than retreat from it. However, the external world merely serves as a reflection of themselves. The Knight of Wands moves towards the external world boldly; the Six of Wands basks in public recognition; and the King of Wands holds command. For the narcissistic type, the world is their stage, and the ego is the main character of the play.

Wands thus belong to the narcissistic/visionary type: the expressive, wilful, and self-defining individual. Fromm's *Exploitative Orientation* transforms, in Porter's terms, into *Assertive-Directing*, the one who leads, creates, and performs. The Knight of Wands is charisma in motion; the Six of Wands is egoic triumph.

The Suit of Pentacles represents a composite libidinal type, what could be called, as Freud posited, the ideal erotic, obsessional, narcissistic blend. Libido is directed toward tangible reality, toward material mastery, bodily care, and emotional dependencies expressed through provision and control. The core need here is for security, independence, satisfaction, order, and for love to be materialised through reliable, tangible, and realistic means like money, gifts, work, and so on. Psychically, this type embodies both the desire to give and be nurtured (erotic) and the need to structure and regulate (obsessional), while also being rooted in the self as a being of growth (narcissistic). The Four of Coins shows the possessive fear of loss, the Six of Coins illustrates the ideal of mutual exchange, and the Page of Coins reflects striving. As Fromm, Porter, and Maccoby elaborated, this type is rightly named the "Marketing" type and the "Flexible-Cohering" orientation: adaptive, responsible, and concerned with balance and reciprocity.

Each suit, then, becomes a libidinal map of character. The therapist will do well to note which suit arises more than others for their client, and which suit the client feels a greater affinity for. Repeating suits or cards can indicate repetition compulsions, unresolved conflicts, or identifications.

THE STRUCTURE OF THE PIP CARDS

As mentioned previously, the pip cards (1–10) represent the minor happenings of life, Waite (1959) himself assuring this meaning. While this does not mean that their significance is debased or "lesser", they are not as grand, mythic, or profound as the Major Arcana.

You will find parallel themes across the common numbers of the suits. The Aces are the pure, unadulterated tone of the card. Twos address either duality or opposition; Fives address conflict; Eights address power and ambition, and so forth. The therapist will do well, in his own studies, to organise his study deck into the different numbers, lay them out before him, and interpret common themes. The therapist will also do well to note which numbers manifest more for a client than others. Their structure makes them sequential, progressive, and combinatory. Thus, they can be read together to form larger meanings.

3.0 Numerical Themes of the Pips

Pip	Theme	Psychoanalytic Functions
Aces	Beginnings	The emergence of self-awareness
Twos	Duality, Imbalance	Object relations; Tensions; Awareness of the 'Other'
Threes	Structure	Triangulation; Symbolic Oedipal Structures; Order.
Fours	Stability	Internalisation of Rules
Fives	Strife	Conflict; Frustration Tolerance; Ego-Superego Tension
Sixes	Success	Reparation; Restitution
Sevens	Effort, Labor.	Reality Principle overcoming Pleasure; Perseverance
Eights	Transformation	Sublimation; Reintegration
Nines	Achievement, Fulfillment	Mastery; Individuation
Tens	Completion	Closure of libidinal stage; Ego maturity; Symbolic resolution.

The table provided above lists the common themes and functions of the pips. The therapeutic meanings are by no means bound dogmatically to this table. Note also that the cards may reflect a lack of the theme itself rather than its attainment, such as the Nine of Swords, for instance.

The pip cards are mostly straightforward in meaning and more easily interpretable. They represent, in most cases, the general unfolding of a certain situation, life stage, or process. Each suit portrays an enclosed system of ten distinct psychic and thematic states. The pips, unlike the court cards, are not personified. Because they portray different scenes, they function more as states of being, unconscious fantasies, or important moments. Unlike the court cards, they are not roles or complexes but states within a process.

THE STRUCTURE OF THE COURT CARDS

Much can be said regarding the significance of the court cards. Firstly, the court cards are the different personifications of the theme of the suit itself. The therapist will do well to sort out each of the court cards thematically and receive the impressions from these suits accordingly.

The Court of Cups reflects the domain of emotion and attachment. Thus, the Court of Cups symbolises the emotional dimension of the family: affection, empathy, and relational harmony (or conflict). The King and Queen represent the parents in their nurturing roles, or their inability to fulfil them. The Knight and Page represent the sensitive child in need. In a clinical atmosphere, they denote issues related to the above, as well as interpersonal dynamics. The therapist will do well to note that if these court cards repeatedly emerge for a client, issues related to early relational experiences, attachment wounds, and sentimental relationships are astir. Themes of love, loss, and empathy may also be present.

The Court of Swords represents the Family of Authority. Within this royal family we see the importance of morality, discipline, and authority. The King and Queen represent the strict demands of parental authority that shape the superego. The Knight and Page are the curious and individuating adolescents whose rebellion is incited by their curiosity, rationalisation, and need for independence. It is clear that this court represents the internalisation of family rules, moral codes of conduct, and defence mechanisms. Clinically, the Court of Swords may signal the therapeutic exploration of internalised authority, superego modification, internal parental voices, anxiety, guilt, defences, and other related themes.

The Court of Wands represents the passionate dimension of the family. This family primarily symbolises power dynamics. Themes of sexuality, assertiveness, competition, conflict, and ambition may be present for the client. The King and Queen are charismatic and strong parental leaders. The Knight and Page are ambitious, explorative, energetic youths. The Court of Wands may denote competition within family dynamics as well as conflict between ego ideals.

The Court of Pentacles represents the Family of Security. As mentioned, the Pentacles represent material security, practicality, and reality. The Court of Pentacles therefore represents the materially secure family, embodying both emotional nurturance and material comfort. This family has mastered both its internal and external realities. The King and Queen provide stability, nurturance, and material assurance. They have instructed their Knight and Page in mastery over their bodily impulses without the need for repression. The Knight and Page then represent the development of autonomy, practicality, bodily awareness, and general competence. In practice, the Court of Pentacles may represent issues related to the above, as well as the anal stage, autonomy versus control, financial anxiety, and groundedness.

Early in this book, I posited that the court cards reflect the Oedipal situation:

KING - QUEEN - KNIGHT

FATHER - MOTHER - SON

As mentioned previously, the King is situated opposite the Knight, with the Queen between them. Waite utilised the Golden Dawn manuscript *Book T* as the source for his formulation of the Tarot. This book was entrusted to him by Samuel MacGregor to use as the original outline of the Tarot. It was exclusive to high-ranking members of the Order.

In his section "The Sixteen Royal Cards", MacGregor, besides identifying the Knight with the Prince and the Knave/Page with the Princess, elaborates a system of the court cards with strong familial overtones. The King is described as the "radix" and "father". The Queen is described as "Mother and bringer-forth". The Prince/Knight is described as "Mighty Son... carried in a chariot... rapid and enduring, yet vain and illusionary unless set in motion by his Father and Mother." The Princess/Page is "The mighty and potent daughter of a King and Queen... combining effects of King, Queen, and Prince."

Waite, pictorially, switched the depiction of the King and the Knight, though the labels and roles remain the same. Waite likely favoured aesthetic probability in this sense, since it is more plausible to see a young man riding a horse than an aged one. Nevertheless, owing to all the above, this is not only a metaphysical or spiritual family but a biological one as well. MacGregor not only elaborates a parental relationship between the King and Queen with the Prince/Knight and Princess/Page, but also a sibling relationship between the Knight and Page. The Knight and Page then, on one level, may represent brother and brother, and on another, brother and sister.

As for the daughter, if we remove the Knight from the situation, we find the following constellation:

KING - QUEEN - PRINCESS (PAGE)

The Queen, in this instance, is situated between the Princess and the King. What makes this distinct from the situation with the son is that the object of affection is not in the centre; rather, it is obstructed by the object of competition. The mother, in the case of the Oedipal situation for the daughter, is at once loved but later despised. During phallicity, the daughter's sexual desires for her father emerge, and the mother is cast away and despised, first for not giving her a penis, and then for being privy to an expression of her father's love that is not hers to own.

The different personages of the court cards are also assigned their proper elements. Kings are associated with Fire, Queens with Water, Knights with Air, and Pages with Earth. Thus, the King of Wands is Fire of Fire, the Queen of Pentacles is Water of Earth, and so on.

The different suits of the court cards therefore represent the Oedipal situation in different manifestations and organisations.

The Court of Cups demonstrates the gentle father who is emotionally receptive and the object of affection for both daughter and son. He is not intimidating during the Oedipal drama and is easily identified with on the part of the son. The Queen, however, while nurturing, is strongly cathected. Though her relational bonds are deep, she may keep the children emotionally dependent on her. The Knight of Cups is the sensitive and romantic son who develops intense romantic ideals about his mother, deeply entrenched in Oedipal longing, idealisation, and sentimental fantasy. The Page is the sensitive daughter who experiences fusion with the father but resents the mother for being the cause of her Oedipal confusion.

The Court of Swords shows us an authoritative father figure, personifying law, morality, and authority. He is the voice of the paternal superego. The Queen is the strict and judgemental mother who establishes high expectations, often at the expense of her children. Her relationship with the King has been equally sharp. As one knows, the more one pushes, the more resistance one faces. Thus, the Knight reflects the rebellious son who actively resists paternal authority. The Princess reflects the observant, withdrawn daughter who internalises rather than combats. She struggles with internalising the mother and is inclined to suffer guilt due to their rivalry. In this court, we see reflected conflicts related to the superego, parental judgements, and morality. The images of this royal family are filled with undertones of anxiety and struggles for autonomy.

The Court of Wands is the closest to the classical Oedipal situation. Firstly, we see a highly elevated image of the father, perhaps even more so than the King of Swords. *Book T* refers to him reverently as "The Lord of the Flame and the Lightning; The King of the Spirits of Fire." He is the masculine and authoritative father, admired for his strength and sexuality. In contrast to the King of Swords, who is purely punitive and condemns sexuality, the King of Wands exercises his sexual authority within the family. He is the admired and envied object of identification for the son and of desire for the daughter.

The Queen is the vibrant and illustrious Oedipal mother. She is the centre of attraction and emotional attachment for the son. The daughter struggles with understanding and accepting her mother's illustriousness, for on one hand she desires to diminish and destroy it, yet on the other she wishes to become like it, thereby resembling her mother in order to attract her father. The Knight (son) is driven by libido, competition, and the unconscious desire to usurp the father and win the admiration of the mother. The Page (daughter) in this suit is overshadowed by the mother's presence and has developed an ambivalent identification with her, as mentioned.

In this passionate family constellation, rivalry, jealousy, and competitiveness abound.

The Court of Pentacles shows the ideal line of libidinal development, akin to what Freud (1961) posited in his *Libidinal Types*. The King is materially stable and practical, providing security, rules, and boundaries while also encouraging comfort and autonomy. He represents mastery over both the internal and external worlds. The Queen is the nurturing and materially secure mother who provides the same for her children. The Knight here strives for autonomy, though not in a rivalrous manner like the Knight of Swords. He seeks purpose, independence, and control. The daughter seeks to establish bodily autonomy and physical competence.

With all this said, I do not suggest that the Court of Pentacles is the "best" among the suits. "Security" is merely a level one reaches at a certain point, and it is often lost as quickly as it is gained. When ill dignified, the Court of Pentacles may represent fixations at the anal level and other conflicts related to anality, also connected with the theme of control. Thus, the need to individuate may transform into the need to dominate, depending on the client.

ACE OF CUPS

The Aces are the embodiment of the element they represent. In other words, they are the pure essence of the suit. Utilising all that has been established, the Ace of Cups symbolises the emergence of the emotional unconscious into consciousness. It depicts the feelings and desires that arise from the unconscious before they are clearly perceived by consciousness. The hand appearing from the clouds symbolises the revelation of unconscious contents into awareness. The overflowing chalice suggests the uncontainable libido within the reservoir of the id.

The cup is a feminine symbol, the inverted triangle (as mentioned earlier) actually being called a chalice. It can represent emotional epiphanies or insights that arise spontaneously, as if "handed" to us. The dove with the Eucharist implies a restorative, healing, or cathartic meaning: that which was repressed has now been discharged. The water lilies imply purification of the unconscious followed by its release.

TWO OF CUPS

The Two of Cups symbolises the culmination of object cathexis in mature romantic relations. Much has already been said regarding this card; thus, I shall keep my exposition here brief. This card represents the union and interplay between the masculine and feminine forces. There is an element of completion and emotional mirroring. The exchange of cups implies mutual emotional nourishment.

This card highlights the phenomenon of projection and identification in a love relation, each seeing themself mirrored in the other. Above and between them hovers a chimera emerging from a caduceus, visually and symbolically recalling the erect phallus. This unique depiction of the caduceus, coupled with the exchange of cups, represents the fusion of love and sex in a mature matrimonial relationship. Desire has been sublimated and elevated, made to "fly". Both man and woman behold each other as if acknowledging the erotic charge between them while remaining within the bounds of emotional dignity.

In the therapeutic context, this card may reflect the integration of sexuality and intimacy. It signifies the moment when emotional attachment and sexual maturation converge. It is therefore fitting that the Golden Dawn referred to this card as "The Lord of Love".

THREE OF CUPS

The Three of Cups, also called *The Lord of Abundance*, depicts the three Graces dancing and celebrating amidst a prosperous harvest. In this image, the three figures are arranged symmetrically in the postural shape of a pyramid. This signifies group cohesion, validation, and recognition arising from belonging.

The three dancing figures, as I discuss in the closing remarks of the suits, represent harmony and emotional resonance within a social or familial group. Here, emotional sharing is not bilateral, as in the Two of Cups, but rather expands outward into the social and external world, revealing the ego's relational development within it.

Regarding the imagery, this is a distinctly feminine card. All the figures are women, and the cups themselves, as well as the element they pertain to, are feminine symbols. The image evokes the earliest psychic experience of a collective maternal upbringing: mothers, aunts, grandmothers, and older sisters who jointly rear the child and provide nurturance and affection. I will elaborate on the element of triangulation in my closing remarks on the suits, but this image depicts precisely the sublimation of competitive or rivalrous impulses into harmony, mutual acknowledgement, and acceptance of the other.

FOUR OF CUPS

I have chosen *The Lord of Blended Pleasure* as the cover and model of this book because it captures both the core atmosphere of psychoanalysis and the use of tarot in psychotherapy. At its core, the Four of Cups depicts an atmosphere of stillness, reflection, inner absorption, and emotional neutrality, all phenomenological occurrences in both the practice of tarot and psychoanalysis. Both disciplines require inward and outward observation, allowing meaning to emerge of its own accord.

It reflects the atmosphere of the analytic space, wherein the therapist holds space for the unconscious of the client to speak. I have identified, on the one hand, the man seated beneath the tree as the analyst himself. This is not the magnificent magician or the imperial charioteer; rather, it is the silent contemplator who sits patiently and permits the unconscious to offer forth its contents. His posture implies that he does not intervene or act; instead, he waits and listens as the client offers him the cup of his joys and sorrows.

The name of the card itself is interesting, namely *Blended Pleasure*. While "Lord", in the sense of the tarot, refers to a ruler or principle governing a particular facet of psychological activity, the phrase *Blended Pleasure* implies a mixture of pleasure with something else. The pleasure in question is present, but not in a pure form. Something is holding it back or inhibiting its full manifestation.

Given the countenance of the man, we can assume this inhibiting emotion to be guilt, boredom, doubt, hesitation, fatigue, or a mixture of all. Pleasure has become joyless, partial, and monitored. The cups lie before the man, but he neither reaches for them nor shows an interest in doing so. This may arise from a fear of disappointment. There is, therefore, a certain anhedonia that emerges when repeated disillusionments lead to indifference towards new experiences.

This is an image of emotional ambivalence, where the subject could take what is being offered but does not. The pleasure offered by the "other" is rejected, and through mistrust, the self remains both self-absorbed and aloof. This is an anal-defensive narcissism, where the child, who is neither giving nor receptive, withholds pleasure and becomes resentful and passive, asserting power in this way. The refusal of pleasure itself becomes pleasurable.

The Four of Cups therefore symbolises withdrawal, apathy, and dissatisfaction, but also contemplation and an inclination inward. It can also represent a defensive withdrawal, wherein the individual retreats into their inner world, triggered by disillusion, disappointment, or regret. This produces a sense of frustration and resistance to pleasure (the cloudy hand).

The figure adopts an inherently defensive body position. His raised shoulders are almost infantile, suggesting a regression to a passive, childlike state of non-compliance with authority. Both the name and the presence of the hand emerging from the cloud imply that, in truth, the figure does desire the experience of pleasure. Perhaps the client who draws this card longs for the perfect escape, the rescue figure, or a hero or heroine who will save them from their present situation.

In actuality, all the strength they need lies within them, for the cloud that emerges in this image is not the same as in the Aces. The cloudy hand that appears in the imagery of the Aces is large and omnipotent. This hand, however, is small in comparison. It represents a kind of auxiliary ego that has come to encourage the ego to carry forth. The crossed arms also imply passive aggression.

The client who identifies with this card must be helped to recognise and confront past and internalised frustrations. They must move beyond their fantasies of idealised fulfilment and, not only actively but realistically, engage with the opportunities that present themselves for growth.

FIVE OF CUPS

Cards Three, Four, and Five of the Suit of Cups represent a fall of pleasure. In the Three, we see the climax; the Four depicts the fall; and the Five depicts the collapse. Hence, the Five of Cups is called *The Lord of Loss in Pleasure*. Pleasure has been utterly lost in this image.

Both the Four and the Five of Cups show cups that the figure refuses to acknowledge. However, what distinguishes the two cards is that in the former there is no loss or spill, whereas in the Five we see two cups of spilt wine and one of water. The subject has lost not only sensual love (wine) but also the primary emotional bond (water). His gaze remains fixed on these three spilt cups because he still identifies with the lost objects.

Though there may be a possibility for future love, hope, and integration, as represented by the two cups behind him, his grief inhibits him from turning around to see them. The ego is therefore trapped in a cycle of rumination and regret, unable to integrate the loss of the beloved object. The tower in the distance symbolises the emotional isolation that accompanies mourning and melancholia. The ego attempts to protect itself through detachment and disconnection from other objects that might inflict the same harm.

One must remember, however far out of sight it may seem, that two cups still remain.

SIX OF CUPS

The Six of Cups symbolises the nostalgia that arises from the innocent memories of childhood. In practice, this card almost always represents early emotional experiences with attachment figures. The cottage behind the old woman evokes the nostalgia of a return to childhood. Defensively, it implies regression. The gentle setting reflects the idealised sense of childhood safety and love.

In therapy, it may also denote the presence of the inner child. When this card appears, it may symbolise the need to resolve childhood desires or memories. It may also represent a need for parental validation, affection, or acceptance, or the need to repair parental relations and make peace with them. In either case, the goal of this card is the attainment of emotional maturity, or pleasure, hence its name *The Lord of Pleasure*.

SEVEN OF CUPS

In this rather intriguing card, which evokes in my mind a sort of circus fair, we see the symbolisation of fantasy, illusion, confusion, and unconscious desire. *The Seven of Cups*, also known as *The Lord of Illusory Success*, symbolises wish fulfilment and the chaotic multitude of unconscious fantasies that compete for conscious recognition. The cups are arrayed with diverse and surreal symbols of power, wisdom, and beauty. Each symbolises an idealised object or impulse of desire such as greed, obsession, or lust. The extravagance of the fantasies within the cups indicates a narcissistic or grandiose aspect.

Ambitious strivings almost always contain within them a hidden sexual striving, and vice versa. In therapy, the card may indicate the use of fantasy as a method of avoidance. Imagination is employed to approach emotional reality. The client may need to explore these different fantasies or projections, differentiating between genuine emotional fulfilment and unrealistic desires. These fantasies should therefore be confronted and clarified. The meanings of this card are, like the cups it depicts, multiplicitous.

EIGHT OF CUPS

The Lord of Abandoned Success symbolises emotional withdrawal and abandonment, as well as the process of personal transformation that occurs when one searches for deeper meaning. On one hand, this card may represent individuation and the pursuit of self-meaning; on the other, it may signify the renunciation of, and departure from, previous emotional attachments for better or worse.

The figure depicted walking away from the *Eight of Cups* has abandoned or renounced them. He has separated himself from previous emotional dependencies or object attachments in pursuit of individuation and personal growth. Mountains in the Tarot often symbolise *"the great work"* or the attainment of human meaning. While this card, on the one hand, may represent the venture towards that goal, it may also signify a depressive withdrawal into the *mountains of the mind*.

The previous pleasures afforded in the former images are consciously recognised as insufficient for complete emotional fulfilment, and the individual must now seek his own. He has gone through pleasure, pain, and compensation, and now realises that he must find satisfaction within himself. As he walks, he faces the *moon*, implying that he is journeying towards it through the mountains. Whereas the sun and the day represent consciousness, the *moon* and the *night*, as established, represent the domain of the unconscious.

He is confronting his repressed emotions, unresolved conflicts, and hidden desires that previously shaped his object relations, as well as his relationship with himself. This is not a journey into the conscious or external world but rather a journey into the *internal and emotional world* – further corroborated by the presence of water.

I find it interesting that the earthen, almost desolate imagery of the *Eight of Cups* follows the dreamy and illusive imagery of the *Seven*. The *Seven of Cups* thus represents fantastical wish-fulfilment, having no base in reality except grandiosity. The *Eight* is what comes after the *fantasy collapses* and the ego becomes disenchanted with the pursuit of pleasure.

In therapy, this card emerges when the client is experiencing trials and tribulations regarding emotional loss and the growth cultivated in letting go. Ultimately, the client is focused on attaining *self-awareness* and a sense of wholeness. Whether on the most optimistic polarity or the most negative, mourning is always present – for one, in this image, mourns the illusion of fantasy.

NINE OF CUPS

I have found the *Nine of Cups*, or *The Lord of Material Success*, to be the most perplexing of all the Tarot cards. As the name and posture of the central figure suggest, this card represents emotional satisfaction, fulfilment, and pleasure. The hitherto wishful desires have now, in actuality, been gratified, and the figure is content with his satisfaction. His posture insinuates even a sort of *narcissism*. This is not an unhealthy narcissism, though, but rather one of pride and confidence.

While emotionally gratifying, it also indicates a defensiveness, as it is the same posture the boy in the *Four of Cups* assumes. Perhaps, even after the journey has been undertaken, he has not completely renounced his narcissism but instead transformed it. This would make sense, given how orderly he has laid his cups upon the adorned table. The arrangement of the cups may reflect his channelling of his impulses into *productivity* and *harmony*. This would then imply a satisfaction of healthy *emotional management* and the fulfilment of *integration*.

I am not, however, as pleased as he is with this interpretation, for I feel as though there is more to this card than I can avail myself of. One gets the impression that something is concealed behind the *drape of the table*. Waite also insinuates this in his *Pictorial Key*. Perhaps the curtain hides the disillusionment of the *Seven* and the pain of the *Eight*. This would then imply that his satisfaction is *false*. Though I find this befitting, I am still not satisfied, and I invite others to explore the meaning of this card.

Perhaps it is this same act of *concealment* which perplexes me, as if he were intentionally tricking me. He stares at me with the gaze of *Mona Lisa*, a *Sphinx-like figure* waiting to see if I answer his riddle. As of now, I am bested.

TEN OF CUPS

"I set my bow in the clouds to serve as a sign of the covenant between me and the earth."

(Genesis 9:13 New American Bible, Revised Edition)

The *Lord of Perpetual Success* represents emotional fulfilment, harmony, and idealised happiness. It signifies successful emotional integration, relational security, self-actualisation, and the fulfilment of psychological needs for emotional nourishment and self-satisfaction. The image portrays a harmonious family, with parents praising the rainbow while children dance and play nearby. It is truly an idyllic image where reality has been elevated to an ideal state.

We can deduce that this is the family of the couple seen in the *Two of Cups*, for the platform, house upon the hill, and clothing motifs are practically identical. One can easily discern the rainbow as a symbol of emotional integration and psychological wholeness. The cups are evenly laid among the bow, representing not only the successful bridging of conscious and unconscious emotional needs, but also the balanced intrapsychic forces. The presence of the children indicates not only maturity but also generational continuity and the task of reproduction.

Therapeutically, this card implies successful integration of emotional experiences, or alternatively, the elevation of reality and expectations to an unrealistic degree.

PAGE OF CUPS
OR THE PRINCESS OF THE WATERS

The *Page of Cups* is a gracious image that represents the spontaneous emergence of unconscious material and thoughts into conscious awareness. This is clearly accentuated by the fish that emerges almost comedically from the cup. He has a childlike character and is rather delicate. He is like a child playing 'pretend', so deeply immersed in reverie that both conscious and unconscious reality are one. He is developing his use of fantasy and creativity.

As a member of the royal cards, he, as established, is more closely related interpretatively to the dimension of the family. He is the vulnerable, sensitive child, emotionally innocent and playful. His smile is innocent, yet behind it is a budding curiosity about sexuality, fantasy, and imagination. He is imaginative, innocent, and seeks love, though often overly impressionable. He represents the youngest child or daughter of the family, who depends on emotional nourishment and familial love.

Recall that the Princes (Knights) and Princesses (Pages) represent children and adolescents navigating familial expectations, oedipal conflicts, psychosexual stages, libidinal desires, and self-development stages in accordance with their suit. The Kings and Queens represent the parental figures within that suit or family. Therapeutically, this card encourages imaginative exploration, creative sublimation, play, and emotional discovery. It may also represent infantile regression. The sixteen court cards have been linked to the sixteen MBTI types, but I shall not go into that in this book.

KNIGHT OF CUPS

The *Knight of Cups* depicts a knight riding forth with a cup extended, symbolising the pursuit of emotional fulfilment, romantic relationships, and idealised emotional goals. This is the active pursuit of unconscious fantasies and idealised love objects. The Knight is searching for someone to whom he can give his cup. He is deeply infatuated with his idealised other. He is of a passionate, intense, and idealistic character. He is the adolescent son in love, a man in touch with his feminine *eros*. Thus, this card symbolises youthful or adolescent emotional impulses.

He is the romantic hero, driven by his desires and idealisations. He is the young man in pursuit of emotionally fulfilling pleasure, in contrast to banal carnal pleasure. Symbolically, he represents the son's romantic *Oedipal fantasies*, driven by libidinal urges toward idealised maternal love objects. This card symbolises the adolescent navigating emerging sexual-emotional desires, romantic fantasies, and Oedipal longings, seeking emotional and erotic fusion.

Therapeutically, it suggests guiding the client toward conscious recognition of their emotional projections, ideals, and fantasies.

QUEEN OF CUPS

The *Queen of Cups* represents the mother as the container of affect. She is the harbour of emotional support and embodies the emotionally responsive mother who is capable of holding and containing the child's complex emotions. Her intense gaze upon the cup implies a deep connection with its contents. I find it interesting that her cup is unlike any other in the entire suit, even different from the one *The Magician* has. Her cup resembles a tabernacle or sacred vessel. She does not drink from the cup; rather, she contemplates it. She is not acting upon the cup; she is containing and preserving what is within it. She is the embodiment of maternal holding.

The closed cup, while it may also represent the womb, symbolises the contents of the emotional life that are hidden and privy exclusively to the inner world. This is why the King, as we shall see shortly, holds a simple cup, for it is not his role to hold but to regulate and act. The Queen, however, must take care not to become overwhelmed by the contents of the cup, lest she be overcome by them and flooded. She must therefore regulate her own emotions as well. This card signals the need to establish emotional boundaries and protect the inner world.

KING OF CUPS

The *King of Cups* symbolises emotional mastery, maturity, and control. He represents mature emotional authority, controlled empathy, and self-regulation, especially on behalf of the father. His strength lies in being nurturing and secure, as well as providing stability amidst tribulation, as seen by the waves, ship, and whale behind him. This is further corroborated by the fact that the King not only holds a cup but a sceptre as well. He and the *King of Pentacles* are the only ones who hold another object besides the symbol of their suit. The *Queen of Wands*, excepting, holds a sunflower.

The cup is a feminine symbol, as established. The sceptre, however, is a phallic symbol. The King holds both because he does not repress emotion, but neither is he ruled by it. He can integrate emotionality with authority and is not overwhelmed by the sea of affect, no matter how turbulent the waters around him may be. He remains *King of the Powers of Water* and is successful at managing anxieties and impulses, providing his children with a healthy template for emotional development. By doing this, he is able to navigate the feminine world of emotions without sacrificing his own masculinity.

This would explain why the *King of Pentacles* and the *King of Cups* hold a sceptre, whereas the *King of Swords* and *King of Wands* do not, for Earth and Water belong to the Feminine, whereas Air and Fire belong to the Masculine. Wands and Swords are phallic and penetrative, and thus the Kings of those suits require no balancing force.

The *King of Cups* is therefore a symbol of emotional masculinity. The *Queen of Wands* is the only Queen of the suits who holds an object other than her symbol. In her hand is a sunflower, bulbous and phallic, as mentioned in my commentary on *The Sun*. She is thus the phallic-erotic mother. She may also reflect the fantasy of the child that the mother possesses all.

Therapeutically, this card addresses sentimental stability and emotional mastery. It may also represent negation regarding personal troubles, for the King, benevolent as he may be, appears almost indifferent to the chaos that surrounds him.

ACE OF SWORDS

The Aces represent the emergence of unconscious contents into consciousness, since they all depict a hand emerging from the clouds, yet the nature of the contents differs among the suits. Though the *Ace of Cups* represents a more sentimental and cathartic emergence, the *Ace of Swords* represents a more forceful intrusion that occurs when previously occulted conflicts and meanings are revealed through the rupture of repressive barriers. The crown and the laurel indicate that this is a triumphant and victorious rupture which ushers in peace and self-mastery, although the sharpness of the sword also suggests a painful or aggressive process.

The Aces themselves are the root of the element and suit in question. The suit of Swords, though often bleak and dreary in imagery, culminates in the completion of a mystery or the closure of a cycle, as seen in the *Ten of Swords*. What must be suffered has indeed been suffered for a higher purpose. Thus, the *Ace of Swords* appears when moments of critical insight or realisation emerge, often amidst difficulty and pain.

TWO OF SWORDS

The *Two of Swords*, or *The Lord of Peace Restored*, is a card of ambivalence, psychological stalemate, and defensive resistance. We see a woman holding two swords firmly across her chest before a scene laden with feminine symbols such as water and the moon. Considering the presence of the swords, which correspond to air, and the water, we see a conflict between the intellect and the sentimental, the conscious and the unconscious, desire and morality.

One is under the impression that she has blindfolded herself from beholding the scene before her, implying either a refusal or an inability to face inner truths, painful emotions, or repressed memories. Blindness also represents castration (Dundes, 2009), and thus she has self-castrated. She blinds herself because to see the truth would destroy the comfort of not recognising. The sea behind her is still, suggesting that repression has worked, yet the moon behind her nonetheless stirs its waves, the contents of her unconscious.

It is for this reason she has cut herself off from the unconscious, driven by fear of its revelations. She has chosen a position of repression, rejection, and defence. The swords are deeply associated with the *superego*, and thus she has internalised her act of self-castration as an injunction of the superego, which says unto her: "Thou shalt not know, thou shalt not see." She is the ego under fearful compliance with the superego.

The Golden Dawn's name for it, *The Lord of Peace Restored*, is therefore very befitting, for the unrest caused by the resurgence of the unconscious has now been 'restored' to peace. She does not realise, however, that beneath the sea dwell all her unconscious conflicts, lying in wait to devour her, as Andromeda before Cetus.

This card may emerge when the client is experiencing ambivalence, blockage, resistance, or self-imposed paradoxes. It emphasises the need to help the client face emotional truths that have previously been avoided in order to attain a sense of *freedom*.

THREE OF SWORDS

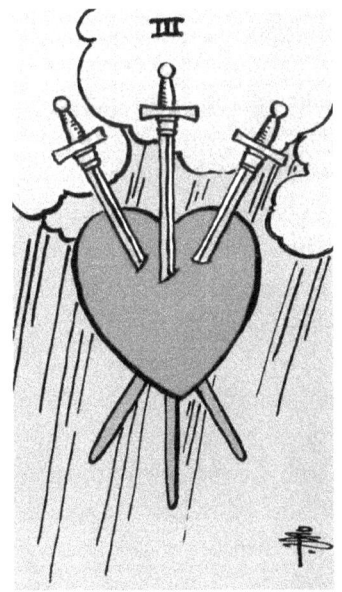

I go much into the significance of the *Lord of Sorrow* at the conclusion of this chapter; therefore, I shall keep what I say herein brief, though there are some elements on which I must elaborate. The significance of the heart as a symbol is associated with the genitals, foetus, womb, and penis, among other sexual and non-sexual associations (Reichbart, 1983). Reichbart likens the beating and palpitations of the heart to the pulsations of the genitals, the sanguineous engorging of the heart to sexual arousal, and the concealment of the heart within the skin to the concealment of the penis within the foreskin.

The piercing of the heart thus evokes castration imagery, which the astute reader shall directly, and with facility, relate to my statements at the end of this chapter. Interestingly, Reichbart also notes that the symbol of the heart is analogous to weapons such as lances and bows, mentioning that the Cupid myth is the sublimation of intense phallic erotic desire. The tip of the weapon thus becomes symbolic of the heart itself, medieval heraldry even substituting the triangular arrowhead for a heart (Wellman, 1886; as cited by Reichbart, 1983). We can, with assuredness, then categorise the sword within this group of weaponised symbolic hearts. Phrases such as "she pierced my heart", "her words impale my heart", "he wounds my heart", and the like naturally come to mind.

The *Three of Swords* naturally depicts rain and a stormy sky, representing mourning, sadness, and depressive states. This card captures both the process of mourning and melancholia as well, for it portrays the bereavement of the lost object. It is one of the few images in the Tarot that does not depict human or animal figures. We are thus in the world of depersonalisation, bleakness, and the incondensable.

This card, beyond the aforementioned, is commonly associated with heartbreak, grief, and relational conflicts, particularly those of an Oedipal nature. For more information regarding this, I again invite the reader to consult my conclusive remarks on the suits, where I elaborate further upon this card.

FOUR OF SWORDS

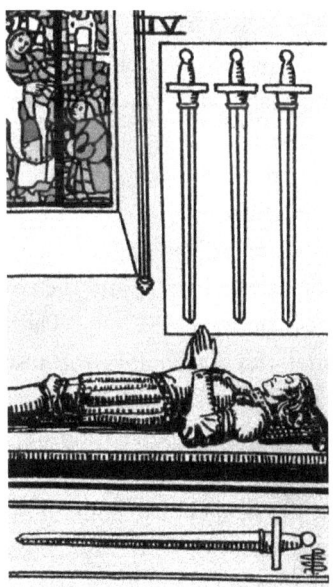

I recall, as a child, when I was first exposed to the images of the Tarot, being utterly perplexed by this image. The pictorial juxtaposition between the three standing swords, the one at rest, he who rests, and the stained-glass figure is profoundly disorienting. It gives the viewer a sense of tension, or rather, an escape from it.

The *Lord of Rest from Strife* represents, from a psychoanalytic viewpoint, the necessity of withdrawal, emotional detachment, contemplation, and psychological incubation. There is an insinuation, both in image and in title, of recovery and isolation, namely psychic restoration after psychological tribulation.

The central figure lies in a posture of peaceful repose, signifying withdrawal, temporary regression, or a hibernation-like state. This represents the psyche's retreat into itself for recuperation and renewal after intense emotional or psychological struggle. Fortune (1927) calls this "The Spheres of Safety," a deep level of psychological submersion akin to absolute hypnosis, wherein the individual separates themselves from reality and enters a state of inaccessible dormition. From without, it appears as though the individual's soul has fled from the body and retreated to a state of safety, as the name suggests.

Psychoanalytically, we can explain this as the flight of the ego from the external world and the complete collapse of bilateral access between the two. The ego, perceiving itself to be under threat, employs the response of flight. Finding itself assailed on all sides and unable to escape, however, it deactivates both perception and interaction and recedes. Fortune writes that this state is inaccessible to any hypnotist, for it lies deeper than consciousness and deeper still than subconsciousness, regarding the escape as nearing a "superconscious" level.

The mechanism of sleep certainly comes to mind, though this defensive retreat is far more severe. It appears akin to a state of dissociation, though curative rather than pathological. From a defensive perspective, it may be seen as an escape into imperturbable reverie, though not an indistinguishable immersion into it, as would occur in psychosis, for instance.

Elaborating further, the setting of a sacred place, church, or chapel-like space alludes to the sense of a psychological sanctuary or a protected inner refuge for healing. This may very well represent the therapeutic space, particularly when hypnoanalysis or hypnotherapy is employed. The couch or resting chair thus becomes parallel to the platform upon which the figure lies. It is a space where the individual can safely process unconscious conflicts, anxieties, and traumas.

The single horizontal sword beneath the resting figure insinuates latent aggression or other unexpressed emotional content. Hostile feelings are kept at bay in order to preserve tranquillity. The three vertical swords hanging above the figure, by contrast, represent those unacceptable feelings that are visible to consciousness, yet currently regarded as inactive or set aside.

This card may emerge when clients require rest, psychological recuperation, or, as the name implies, escape from strife. Hypnosis or imaginal work may be called for. The client must be encouraged to utilise reflective self-awareness while remaining mindful of the differences between retreat, rest, and confrontation.

FIVE OF SWORDS

The *Lord of Defeat* depicts a rather ambiguous scene between three gentlemen, one of whom appears to be in an advantageous mood in contrast to the other two. We get the impression that the man at the forefront is behaving discreetly, cautious so as to avoid alerting the two men before him. He holds three swords in his hands and proceeds to pick up two from the ground, which we can deduce belong to the other two men. The *Five of Swords* thus symbolises conflict, rivalry, and humiliation, particularly those arising from power struggles. It portrays the dynamics of aggression, competition, defeat, and domination. Psychoanalytically, we can observe themes of narcissistic injury and interpersonal conflict.

The central figure beholds his defeated opponents with satisfaction, as if having finally balanced a score with them after much built-up resentment. He asserts his superiority at their expense. The psychology of narcissism is aptly applied here. The other two figures lament in humiliation and despair, representing the defeat that accompanies interpersonal humiliation or narcissistic injury. The swords, pertaining to the element of Air, frequently contain imagery of clouds. The clouds in this image, however, are dark and stormy, suggesting emotional turbulence. The sea once again appears, representing the unconscious factors at play in the enactment of narcissistic and interpersonal dilemmas. The swords, unquestionably, represent conflict and injury.

Themes of aggression, splitting, relational dynamics, and narcissistic vulnerabilities are recalled when the *Five of Swords* emerges in the therapeutic space.

SEVEN OF SWORDS

The *Lord of Unstable Efforts* depicts a man running away discreetly from a scene with five swords in his hand. It seems quite an effort to carry them in such a manner, so he leaves two behind. Interpreted literally, this image is a depiction of theft. What distinguishes the theft depicted in the *Five of Swords* from that in the *Seven of Swords* is that the former is carried out successfully and with the venom of betrayal, whereas the latter is done at a loss, with no lasting success despite momentary satisfaction. There is a compromise involved in the theft that transpires in the *Seven*, whereas in the *Five* there is only gain on the part of the thief.

The thief has stolen swords from the military camp. His former confederates appear farthest to the left in the background, beneath the points of the swords. Though they seem unsuspecting and at rest, as indicated by the cloud emerging from them, which might suggest a bonfire, when they return and find both their resources and ally missing, they shall surely come to an accurate conclusion regarding the culprit. We can deduce that they will hunt him down and pay eye for eye, or in this case, sword for sword. The meaning of "Unstable Effort", therefore, is clarified.

The *Seven of Swords* symbolises deception, secrecy, and manipulation, namely psychological evasion. This image, as mentioned, demonstrates deceit, cunning, and avoidance of responsibility or truth. The figure carrying the swords looks behind him with what appears to be a mixture of both caution and culpability. While this card in divination represents the presence of hidden agendas, it also represents defences utilised to avoid self-honesty. The cautious glance therefore represents the paranoia that accompanies avoidance. Bearing these in mind, we can deduce that the thief, in this moment, is experiencing anxiety borne of his guilty conscience. Paranoia is guilt projected outward; therefore, his vigilant countenance betrays his fear.

The encampment itself may represent the truths from which he is running, but also the unresolved relational dynamics against which he has reacted. They are the emotional complexities from which he is distancing himself. There is an internal and external contrast in the man; despite being internally assailed by paranoia, he manoeuvres it with delicacy and poise. The actual act of tiptoeing away quietly betrays his vulnerability as he escapes and employs his avoidant defences. The scattered swords represent the fragmented truths of the matter. Though his evasions have afforded him momentary calm, they will not do so for long. This therefore represents a selective acknowledgement of psychic truths and realities, a state of partial self-awareness and partial self-denial.

When this card emerges, and more so when it is identified with, one can suspect the presence of defence mechanisms such as rationalisation, intellectualisation, or avoidance, used to deflect emotional truths or interpersonal conflicts. Guilt, paranoia, and anxiety should be explored as well. The client must be guided towards emotional honesty and responsibility.

EIGHT OF SWORDS

The striking image of the *Lord of Shortened Force* immediately incites feelings of melancholy, entrapment, and pity. It is perhaps because of this that I most often see this card emerge for clients (especially women) struggling with addiction (besides *The Devil*), or even more so in cases of narcissistic or domestic abuse. I frequently observed identifications with this image during my time as a drug and alcohol counsellor, where both of the aforementioned were present in many female clients simultaneously. The *Eight of Swords* symbolises psychological entrapment, powerlessness, and victimisation, though this oppression may be imposed by both external and internal forces. In the latter case, it may also symbolise masochism, learned helplessness, internalised guilt, and psychological binding.

The seven swords encircle the bound woman, clearly signifying psychological entrapment and paralysis. She may be confined by external prohibitions and actual dangers, but also by internalised prohibitions, irrational fears, repression, and anxiety. These can themselves form a kind of self-imposed entrapment that prevents her from achieving liberation of expression. Whether she is bound by external forces or by a repressive and sadistic superego cannot be stated so simply. The blindfold appears once again in this image, last seen in the *Two of Swords*. We must therefore observe the contrast between the two images if we wish to understand its significance more profoundly.

At once, one notices the presence of the blindfold in both images. The blindfold, as mentioned both by myself and by Dundes (2009), is a symbol of castration and the punitive function of the superego. The blindfold motif appears only in these two images of the Tarot. Not even *Justice* is depicted as blindfolded. In the *Eight of Swords*, the woman is not only bound tightly with bands around her torso and arms, but she is also left exposed to the elements, standing in water and muddy earth. In the *Two*, the subject still retains a degree of agency and mastery. In the *Eight*, the subject is completely stripped of autonomy and cut off from the ego ideal (the castle). The *Eight* introduces what the *Two* lacks: the element of binding. She has not only been blindfolded but restrained as well. Thus, not only can she not see (know), but she also cannot move (act). She has forfeited her phallic aspect entirely and has been prohibited by the eight swords from desiring and disobeying.

What is interesting is that the bodily posture of the woman in the *Ten* is open despite the bindings, whereas in the *Two* it is closed, yet unbound. Moreover, the swords that encircle her are only partly enclosing. She could, in theory, leave, but the authority of the superego is far too strong, and the threat of punishment for eating of the forbidden fruit is far too terrifying. This is therefore the portrait of a neurotic ego overwhelmed by the anxiety of guilt and fear. She has been banished from the castle (paradise, power, sexuality, masculinity) and is now in a state of feminine masochism. She has accepted passivity and punishment as her role.

She has identified with the castrated position. It is for this reason that these two images, though not that of *Justice*, are depicted as blindfolded. *Justice* has seen, accepted, and imposed the law. She is post-oedipal, for she has passed through the fires of desire without neurosis. The woman of the *Eight* knows very well but refuses to acknowledge the truth that would cause her pain. The depiction of lack, submission, and inferiority is conveyed even numerically, the *Two* and *Eight of Swords* being of lesser value than *Justice* (10).

What distinguishes her position in the *Two* and the *Eight* is that, in the former, the blindfold appears to be voluntary. She is in a controlled posture, suggestive of preserved equilibrium. She refuses to look because doing so would destroy the illusion of peace, preferring not to acknowledge consciously the serpent that already roams and slithers within her garden. She chooses repression as a defensive manoeuvre and is the agent of it.

In the latter card, its imposition is accompanied by accepted helplessness. She has forsaken compromise and now surrenders to the superego. The ego is no longer in a state of negotiation, but of paralysis. The woman is surrounded by phallic swords, yet she cannot wield them. In the *Two*, the swords are harnessed and mastered by the subject. In the *Eight*, the swords harness and master the subject herself. In the former, the woman holds back her instincts through the modulating function of the ego, whereas in the latter, not only can she hold nothing (her defences), but she has become the subject of her very prohibitions.

Both cards represent a paralysis of some kind. However, in the *Two* this paralysis arises from ambivalence, whereas in the *Eight* it arises from submission to the superego. As the name *Shortened Force* implies, desire itself has been shortened, not eliminated, but diminished into masochism. Another connecting factor between the *Two* and the *Eight* is the depiction of water. Though in one this water is abundant and serene, in the other it has dried up and been replaced by mud and barren earth. I mentioned in my exposition that the water in the *Two of Swords* contains within it the repressed sexual contents of the woman. In the *Eight*, the woman has chosen to dive into the waters of the unconscious and to know, but now faces the consequences of knowing. There is no more serenity or feminine beauty, only bleakness and shame. The libido has become dammed up and no longer flows towards Eros, creativity, love, and life. The psyche cannot move forward and is now bound by repetition, left with a sterile unconscious and a miserable existence.

Perseus Frees Andromeda - Wtewael Joachim (1615)

I previously likened the woman in the *Two of Swords* to Andromeda. In mythological paintings, Andromeda is also depicted as bound, though to a rock rather than to swords. I mentioned in my exposition that the woman in the *Two of Swords* is an Andromeda-like figure who is ignorant of what lies beneath the sea behind her. In the *Ten of Swords*, she has fallen prey to what lay beneath the surface of the waters, to the repressed.

Perhaps, then, the myth of Andromeda provides illumination regarding what the woman in the *Ten* requires in order to be free. Having established the aforementioned, I deduce that she needs to integrate her masculine sexuality into her feminine sexuality. The princess Andromeda has been depicted as nude since antiquity (Barker, 2021). This nude form of Andromeda was embraced by artists of the Renaissance, Early Modern, and Modern periods. This naked depiction of Andromeda, which prevailed over the clothed variants, therefore may confirm the erotic undertones of the story.

1st Century, BC, Depiction   *Andromeda ~ Gustave Doré (1869)*

The nude Andromeda, having forsaken her masculine desire, has surrendered to the monstrous superego. If she successfully abandons her immersion in masochistic femininity and accepts her masculine Eros, she may yet preserve herself from being consumed by the forces of the unconscious. Perhaps, then, the woman of the Tarot requires Perseus to come and rescue her. This can represent her own healed and transfigured inner masculine force, or the salvific father.

In mythology, Andromeda is offered by her mother and

father to the sea monster as punishment for their pride. Their pride, however, stemmed from their praises of Andromeda's beauty, elevating her above even the daughters of Neptune. For brevity, this comes with consequences, and Andromeda is offered as appeasement. The main concern of the Andromeda–Perseus narrative, then, lies in her beauty, her sexuality.

When Perseus rescues Andromeda, he has just slain Medusa and is now venturing to free her. Perseus, having slain the castrating and phallic mother, has triumphed over his Oedipal complex and proceeds to rescue the mature love object, the sexual woman. She, whose sexuality has been bound by both society and, consequently, her psychic world, is freed by he who desires her and allows her to express her restrained desire with him.

The Knight Errant ~ John Everett *Ruggiero Rescuing Angelica ~ Gustave Doré*

(1870) *(1881)*

The motif of the bound woman appears in several stories. In art, for instance, John Everett Millais in his *The*

Knight Errant (1870) depicts a knight loosening a naked woman with his sword from her bond to the tree. Her averted gaze indicates shame or conscientiousness, for he beholds her nakedness. The tree to which she is tied recalls the Tree of Knowledge of Good and Evil, symbolically likening her to Eve. Yet her loosened hair implies the presence of sexuality. She may neither feel this sexuality, as indicated by the bind around her abdomen, nor act upon it, as indicated by the bind around her wrists. She is prohibited from masturbation and from attaining sexual gratification of her own accord, lest she suffer shame and punishment. The knight, therefore, comes to allow her to express her sexuality with him, provided he both participates in it as the dominant force and is the recipient of her desire. The act of feminine bondage and masculine release in these narratives is a clear depiction of the sexual dynamic: the woman is bound in a passive state and then freed by the desirous man.

The interplay between feminine masochism and masculine sadism is obvious. This element of sadomasochism is visually apparent in Everett's painting. He is armoured and concealed, whereas she is nude and vulnerable. Each individual seems careful in beholding the other. The man is cautious, lest his bestial sexuality be awakened, while the woman is bound for that very reason. The act of serving and rescuing her, then, liberates him from the guilt of desiring her – and vice versa. This is the source of the fetishistic, voyeuristic element one senses when beholding these images. The voyeurism functions as a distancing from desire, while still allowing them to 'appropriately' indulge in it. The young man, therefore, engages in his sexuality under the guise of morality. Ultimately, she is the libidinal desire (either of the man himself or within herself) liberated. Her beauty (sexuality), once subdued by the impositions of the superego, is now freed by the man's desire. The blindfolded woman in the *Eight of Swords* as a symbol of castrated feminine sexuality is, therefore, reinforced.

Doré's depiction of Angelica, though similar to *The Knight Errant*, is closer to the depiction of the Andromeda story. Angelica is the subject of the piece, bright and illuminated. The repressed has returned to consume her. Ruggiero seems to shield his eyes from beholding her, again preventing the primitive desire from awakening within him, for he is indeed armoured and restrained. The serpentine, phallic monster that threatens both Angelica and Ruggiero embodies the ancient terror of unregulated sexual desire.

Munich (1989) views the moment before the hero rescues the maiden as the "final test of manhood" before the transition into adult male sexuality. She interprets *The Knight Errant* as a depiction of assault rather than desire. I reply that the 'assault' is itself desired, though I opine that it is not the principal element of the piece.

Saint George and the Dragon - Paolo Uccello (1470)

Even the myth of Saint George is connected to the Hero Rescuing Bound Maiden motif. Artists psychologically conflated these myths, due to their unconscious resonance, to the point where most artistic depictions of Perseus, as provided herein, show him riding a horse, though in classical myth he is said to have used the winged sandals of Mercury (Whatley et al., 2004). It goes without saying that the Christianised myth of Saint George is certainly the most sublimated of all the rescue stories. *Sleeping Beauty* by Walt Disney may also be aptly categorised here. In all depictions, the young man is shown thrusting his phallic weapon into the monster, thereby rescuing the woman. He, the phallic saviour, has slain the castrating monster (mother) and has reclaimed the feminine object. The threat of consumption by the beast in myth and fairytale is, according to Warner (as cited by Marilynn & Pamela, 2003), a metaphor for sex. This makes sense, not only because of my aforementioned analyses, but also because, in the Apocalypse, the Woman of Revelation, identified in Roman Catholic theology with Mary, is rescued by God from the threat of consumption. Thus, Mary's virginity is saved from the threat of sexual desire by the intervention of God.

Perseus Rescuing Andromeda - Giuseppe Cesari (1594-95)

Departing from my elaborate, though necessary, digression, the image of the *Ten of Swords* has thereby been deepened. Therapeutic themes of victimisation, masochism, abuse, repression, and helplessness are obvious, as are those of liberation, self-expression, emotional autonomy, and empowerment. The latter point is substantiated by the fact that, despite all her tribulation, Andromeda was placed among the stars.

NINE OF SWORDS

The intensity of the suit of Swords does not end with the Eight but continues into *The Lord of Despair and Cruelty*. This image is one of bottomless anxiety, guilt, despair, and torment. The card depicts intense rumination, superego persecution, intrusive guilt, and severe psychic pain and anguish.

The nine swords that hang above the figure represent the severe and punitive functions of the superego. Note that the Nine of Swords has no finite point or end. This could imply that the anguishes of the individual exist perpetually in the mind and/or that the disaster over which they lament has ongoing consequences. The figure, depicted in a state of overwhelming anxiety and self-condemnation, embodies the ego under attack by the superego. We see, therefore, a depiction of depressive guilt, pathological anxiety, and profound shame. The darkness that encompasses the figure is the darkness of the ego in which it finds itself. The figure on the bed suggests the torment of nightmares as a symptom of the aforementioned. The carving beside the bed is of Cain and Abel. This depiction of Cain and Abel represents the internal drama between the ego and the superego. For further discussion regarding Cain and Abel, I refer the reader to my book *The Cain Complex*. In therapeutic contexts, all that has been mentioned should be explored with the client, along with unconscious fears, repressed memories, unresolved traumas, and the need for self-compassion and emotional support.

TEN OF SWORDS

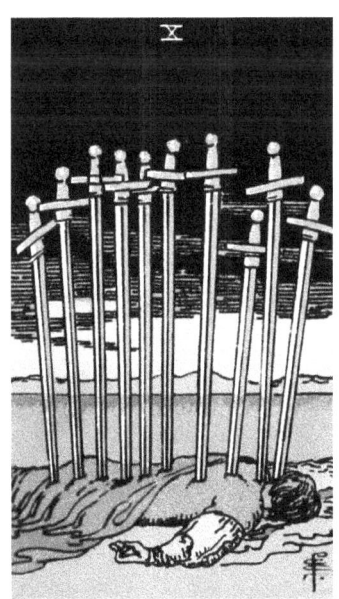

The intensity of the suit reaches its culmination in *The Lord of Ruin*. The *Ten of Swords*, at first glance, is a symbol of psychological crisis, annihilation, and breakdown. The impression one receives is of total ego collapse and defeat. One witnesses the victim of internalised aggression, betrayal, and self-destruction. The impalement of the individual by the ten swords represents the destruction of the ego caused by the collapse of defence mechanisms under overwhelming psychological strain, as in the case of suicide. The ego surrenders to its self-directed aggression and commits self-murder. The blood mingling with the red cloth symbolises profound psychological trauma. Suffering has transpired. The dark sky drawing nigh represents profound depression, abandonment, emptiness, and psychological darkness.

Despite the despair portrayed herein, however, a hidden detail in this card reveals a central component of its message. The figure, if one notices, faces the rising sun, and his index and middle fingers, along with his thumb, are in the position of a pontifical blessing. What at first appears to be a depiction of utter defeat and desolation soon becomes a depiction of fulfilment. In truth, a mystery has been completed. What has been suffered was suffered for a higher purpose. The impalement of the ten swords, therefore, becomes Christ-like. Something new and grand is being ushered in through suffering. Transformation follows the ending. The sorrow and burdens of the entire suit have been redeemed and, at the end of the rosary of sorrows, the glorious mysteries have been attained. For the man in the image, hope remains.

In a clinical context, this card emerges when clients experience a profound psychological crisis, emotional despair, or depressive breakdown. Positively, it emphasises the necessity of collapse for psychic renewal. During such times, clients must be carefully guided through their despair in order to foster the emergence of strength, growth, and healing.

PAGE OF SWORDS
OR THE PRINCESS OF RUSHING WINDS

The *Lotus of the Palace of Air* generally symbolises intellectual curiosity, idealism, and emerging mental awareness. During adolescence, the young individual becomes increasingly aware of themselves and the world around them, and if well acquainted with their libido, they become imbued with romantic idealism. The prominently held sword symbolises the emergence of rational and intellectual thought. The windswept hair and flowing clouds further signify mental activity, especially turbulence or powerful thoughts. His imbalanced posture suggests internal conflict or uncertainty regarding what lies ahead, as well as immaturity. His facial expression conveys alertness, hypervigilance, or the negated uncertainty of adolescence. The turbulence that surrounds him may naturally accompany his increasing individuation, identity formation, and self-awareness. The birds in the sky imply the yearning for individuation, freedom, and adulthood, the latter being understood as liberation from the oppressive tyranny of the parents.

The *Page of Swords* represents the watchful observer and the anxious child of the court of Swords. She is the daughter who learns about rules, logic, and familial expectations, while also experiencing anxiety about meeting them. She also symbolises the formation of defence mechanisms through parental influence within the authoritative family of Swords.

Therapeutically, the *Page of Swords* emerges when the client is in a phase of intellectual growth or heightened self-awareness. It may signal the exploration of adolescent identity and the fostering of emotional maturity. The importance of aspirations and identity formation may also be addressed.

KNIGHT OF SWORDS

KNIGHT of SWORDS.

It seems as though all the hostility contained within the suit of Swords is expressed in the *Knight of Swords*. In this image, we find a knight with his sword upraised, charging across a vale almost haphazardly. He symbolises swiftness in action, assertiveness, and impulsivity. Psychoanalytically, this card portrays acting out, aggression, manic defences, impulsive drives, and the pursuit of control or dominance.

His raised sword may symbolise analytic dominance, aggression turned outward, or internal control over anxiety and fear. The horse charging forward is undeniably representative of his intense sexual drives, emotional intensity, and relentless mental urgency. His reckless mastery over the horse reinforces acting-out behaviours as a means of escaping depressive anxieties, vulnerability, and fear. The windswept clouds appear again in this image, yet in a more chaotic fashion than before. These represent the same qualities as in the *Page*, though in a more severe form.

His heavy armour refers to his defences, concealing vulnerability or weakness. I have spoken much regarding the *Knight of Swords*, since he plays a part in my psychosexual sequence of the Tarot, so I will keep familial interpretations brief. The Knight is *The Crusader*, the aggressive and impatient son driven by righteousness and ideals. He charges forward, either in rebellion or in the embodiment of the father's masculine expectations. He either challenges or represents paternal authority, though it is possible to be both simultaneously. He has internalised the authority of the father and either rebels against it or integrates it into his own pursuits.

Themes of defensive aggression, the pursuit of destiny, and impulsiveness are associated with the therapeutic dimensions of this card. Clients can be guided towards healthier emotional engagement and the overcoming of emotional impulsivity.

QUEEN OF SWORDS

QUEEN of SWORDS.

The *Queen of Swords* is one of the images that appears most frequently in my work with female clients. I often find associations made either with themselves as single or supported mothers who must carry on alone, or with their hostile and detached mothers.

The *Queen of the Thrones of Air* is the embodiment of critical detachment and moral judgement. As discussed elsewhere, she is the castrating or persecutory mother. She is the harsh maternal superego who watches, judges, and punishes deviations from familial standards. She is the introjected voice of the mother who loves conditionally. Her raised hand beckons the child forward, as if to say, "Thou mayest approach me, yet only if thou satisfy me." The sword held upright facilitates this arbitrary power. It is not a sword of action but of judgement. The throne is adorned with the face of a cherub, symbolising the omnipresent and all-powerful mother who ever observes and never embraces. Because of her incessant internal presence, the child remains under continual pressure, experiencing scrutiny and perfectionism through self-surveillance.

The solitary bird flying above is a clear representation of isolation, though it may also signify sovereignty and the yearning for freedom. It expresses the client's hope and aspiration to break free.

It is not uncommon for the Queen to be mistaken for a King. For this reason, I suggest that nameless versions of the cards be used with clients, provided the practitioner can still identify them. It is important that the client does not feel inhibited in their projections onto the card. This helps to prevent both unconscious and conscious filtering.

One adolescent female client of mine described the *Queen of Swords* as "bossy, yet powerful." A little girl narrated that "the Queen is mad at one of the servants who was talking about her." Another adolescent female client told me, under hypnosis, that she saw the face of her critical mother in the guise of the *Queen of Swords*. Several single mothers told me that they saw themselves in the *Queen of Swords*, either in relation to their resentment towards their husbands (or ex-husbands) or in their current strivings towards personal assertion and strength. Interestingly, Waite, in his *Key*, wrote that the sword, while not representing mercy, is scarcely a symbol of strength. He associated the meanings of this card with widowhood, sadness, separation, and malice.

Utilising the feedback of several of my clients, in addition to the aforementioned, we see the presence of maternal identifications with the phallic mother who possesses power. She is not pleased by any penis, because she herself wields one. The *Queen of Swords* as a mother is not a nurturing presence – she is simultaneously desired and feared for her power.

The associations of this card with the judgemental mother who demands perfection are clear. Likewise, the associations expressed by my clients reveal that this image reflects the experience of feminine authority as bound to sorrow and emotional isolation. In the *Queen of Swords*, love has been transformed into law. She is the emblem of women who have had to become self-sufficient at the cost of tenderness. Themes regarding the image of the internal mother are unmistakable.

KING OF SWORDS

As mentioned across this book, the *King of Swords* represents the paternal superego. I shall not delve profoundly into the significance of this image, since it has been interpreted numerous times – however, I shall say that the *King* shares in the detachment and coldness of the *Queen*. He is the strict and authoritative father who executes and enforces the paternal law. He is the father of discipline, authority, and reason. When this symbol emerges for the client, it implies psychological restraint and rigidity. It also implies dominance over the psyche via inflexible moral standards, objective detachment, and logic. On the other hand, however, it may signal the mastery of the themes found in the suit of *Swords* – whether they have been attained or are to be attained in the approximating phase of psychological work.

ACE OF WANDS

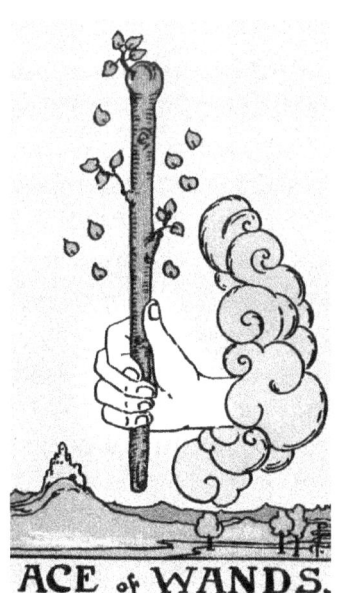

The *Root of the Powers of Fire* symbolises sexual potency, vitality, creativity, and libidinal strength. Even the sexual and passionate connotation of the name should be obvious. As is common among the aces, this card likewise depicts an emergence. The emergence in question is the bringing forth of unconscious desires, primary drives (especially sexuality and creativity), and the awakening of instinctual energy that fuels personal growth. The upright, bulbous wand is overtly phallic. The imagery of the erect phallus is obvious. There is a masturbatory implication in this card, where the hand that emerges from the cloud produces leaves and pleasure of its own accord. The leaves sprouting upon the wand symbolise the transformation of pure libidinal impulses into sublimated creative endeavours. The wood of the wand is alive, not dead – thus, there is generation, not degeneration. The growing leaves insinuate the hormonal transformation of the phallus of the young boy into manhood (i.e. pubertal transformation).

The distant landscape with the castle represents personal goals and unconscious aspirations, which, as mentioned before, almost always contain a sexual component beneath. The castle is the symbol of the home, since this is where the *Royal Family* live. One may delight in regarding this as the abode of the *Court of Wands*. In fairy-tales and dreams, the castle atop the hill often represents the goal of the hero – where the princess sleeps or is entrapped. Its presence upon a hill, however, indicates that it is not easily reached, and challenges must be confronted before she is rescued. It is thus the *Oedipal* area where the son must battle the dragon, evil stepmother, or wizard who blocks him from his love object. It is, then, the destination of the libido (recall my elaboration of the *Eight of Swords*).

In therapeutic contexts, the *Ace of Wands* emerges when clients experience, or are nigh a spontaneous awakening of, creativity, sexual desires, instinctual energies, or vitality. It signals the need to explore these elements so as to stimulate psychological growth and rejuvenation. It also heralds the approach of ambition and striving. The client must take care with megalomaniac, sadistic, or narcissistic feelings that arise.

TWO OF WANDS

The *Lord of Dominion* provides us with a view of the scene in which the *Ace of Wands* takes place, as seen from the perspective of the castle. We can see hills and bodies of water similar to those depicted surrounding the castle in the prior image. Here, the creative and ambitious strivings have been refined and channelled. The individual, who appears student-like, holds a globe in his hand and contemplates the horizon – or the future possibilities that lie before him. The libido, once undirected, has now begun to be consciously harnessed and directed. The globe he holds connotes the narcissism and desire to master the world around oneself that arises when these strivings are channelled.

The ego, seeking mastery, exploration, and dominance of both the internal and external world, begins to regard it as something to be tamed. The ego, caught between the impulses of the unconscious and rational, conscious strivings (the two wands), stands between them and negotiates. The rather ornate and attractive formal robes he wears represent the formulation of the personality – that which is constructed when the individual forms an identity with which to dress the ego. Waite identified the emotion of this image as "the sadness of Alexander amidst the grandeur of this world's wealth." The ego ultimately comes to accept that it shall never possess the entire globe it holds upon its hand and realises the futility of vanity.

This image emerges when themes of personal expansion, identity formation, and aspirational conflict arise. As is typical of the *Two's*, the individual who identifies with this image must find balance between emotional and rational strivings. Waite's description of the emotion in this image implies that, though the land before the figure lies in wait for his conquest, he is missing one thing – love. Fire is opposed to water; thus, *Wands* are opposed to *Cups*. There is a lack of the feminine, of otherness, and of sentimental tenderness seen within that suit.

Though the field is wide and vast, no one else is seen.

His melancholy is akin to the post-*Oedipal* recognition that the mother (or object of desire) can never truly be completely owned, as is portrayed in *Venus and Adonis*. The name *Lord of Dominion* then poses a paradoxical question: what is his dominion, and is he truly its lord? The ego is not the master of its house, nor is it ever truly the master of the external world. The "sadness of Alexander" shown herein, then, is a depiction of this very realisation.

THREE OF WANDS

What strikes one when observing the *Lord of Established Strength* from an interpretative perspective is that both he and the *Lord of Dominion* gaze outward upon a vast field.

Indeed, both figures gaze outward, but the emotional impression of each image, though similar, nevertheless differs. Sequentially, these two images portray distinct stages of psychic development in relation to the attainment of the object of desire.

The *Lord* in the *Two of Wands* gazes out upon the open plain and contemplates the world, rather than desiring it. He does not look upon the land with hope, but with melancholy. We can hear him ask himself, "Is that all there is?" He speaks in the voice of the client who "has it all" yet remains dissatisfied, as if an inaccessible aspect of the self were nevertheless vacant.

The *Lord of the Three of Wands*, however, has now not only opened himself to the world (for he does not reside in a castle, but upon a cliff) and gazes forward toward the world, the future, and the other. The world is seen as one of possibility. Sequentially, this card depicts the evolution of the striving for mastery to the striving for individuation, as discussed in greater detail in the concluding remarks on the suits. The *Lord of Established Strength* moves away from narcissistic mastery and into the process of mature individuation. The subject has obtained the wand handed to him in the *Ace*, descended from the castle of the *Two*, and now steps out into the world in order to become.

This sense of individuation thus explains the name *Established Strength*. It is not a reference to external power or success, but to the establishment of inner strength.

FOUR OF WANDS

The *Lord of Perfected Work* symbolises the moment when the libido, once invested in imagination, fantasy, or expectation, is now fully actualised. Principally, it represents the movement from individuation into interdependence with a romantic other. In this image, we see what appears to be a wedding celebration, though Waite describes the figures as two women.

Sequentially, this card depicts the young man who, once within the realm of the home, has now gone out into the world and achieved individuation of his own – delighting in his marriage and the commencement of the edification of his own family. The meaning of this image is rather straightforward. It reflects positive libidinal energy, emotional satisfaction, secure attachment, and healthy integration.

When this card emerges in psychotherapy, it can signal either the achievement or the need for these qualities, as well as emotional intimacy and acceptance. *Perfected Work* thus implies that the process of individuation has been perfected through relational attainment.

FIVE OF WANDS

This card, quite befittingly, is called the *Lord of Strife*. It portrays five individuals, either at war or at play. Though Waite seems to have intentionally made this visually ambiguous, the title indicates otherwise. The number five likewise belongs to Mars, so the aggressive dimension of this card is brought forward rather than the playful. Hence, it represents psychic conflict, rivalry, and emotional tension.

It brings to mind a group of siblings gathered together – whose play is mixed with joy and hatred. Perhaps it is this symbolic parallel to siblings at play that causes the ambiguity of the card. Individually, it represents the inevitable conflict that arises when the libido, once harmoniously directed, becomes frustrated and struggles for self-assertion. The multiple figures at odds with one another may represent the intrapsychic structures likewise at odds and competing for psychic dominance.

The juxtaposition of the fertile and barren land depicts the split between the conscious and unconscious domains of internal life. The emergence of, or identification with, this card illuminates themes of conflict, rivalry, fragmentation, and aggression. It incites the exploration of sibling rivalry and the re-establishment of harmony.

SIX OF WANDS

The *Lord of Victory*, I opine, is the most enigmatic image of the entire Minor Arcana. It depicts a rather handsome cavalier riding triumphantly upon his vested horse, accompanied by his entourage who celebrate him. He wears a laurel wreath, and upon his wand is another.

His is the image of achievement, direction, and, as the name suggests, victory. This is not a personal or intimate victory as in the *Four of Wands*, but rather a very open and public one. The individual has grown; the external world responds to his growth, and others react. The ordinary others now applaud the exalted ego who dwells among them. The achievements of the ego are on display to the external world, which, in turn, validates and affirms it.

He is now heroic and admirable, recognised as having "made it". He is the older brother who, once entangled in the family drama, transcends it through identification with the victorious father and garbs himself in the form of the ideal ego. He possesses the adorned phallus and is now revered by his younger siblings – particularly his younger brothers, who both envy him and wish to become like him, spurred on by the praises directed toward their brother by those around them who urge them to "be like him". The *Lord of Victory* also denotes sexual conquest and triumph.

Despite the seeming positivity and joy of the name and image of the card, there are latent and hidden tensions depicted as well – tensions that may not be obvious upon first glance. Every tarot card has a hidden meaning or a warning. The warning in this card lies both in what is concealed beneath the seemingly exaggerated drapery of the horse and in the hidden face behind the cavalier.

The horse is a symbol of sexual drive and the *id* (Freud, 1965). Therefore, there is a secret sexual conquest or desire that is cloaked by social acceptability or morality. His public triumph conceals a hidden, perhaps shameful victory – likely sexual in nature. One recalls the ostentatious weddings of closeted homosexuals who, after marrying much later in life, are seen as having "made it" within the family. After much tension and doubt regarding his sexuality, he finally marries far later than his contemporaries, and the family experiences a moment akin to: "See? I knew he wasn't gay. I knew he would marry eventually."

Is the celebration for him, or for his projected self? The grandiose implications of this image are obvious. The sinister face behind him is that of the jealous sibling rival. It is the *Cainitic* sibling who looks upon the victories of his brother with contempt and scorn. This hidden, seemingly mature face evokes the figure of the elder sibling who, quietly resentful and masking their hatred, observes the younger sibling's triumph. Dundes (2009) notes that in myth and in fairytales, the youngest sibling is commonly portrayed as the hero.

Alice is a younger sibling, so is Cordelia, and Gretel, among many others. Rivalry against siblings is formed from the emotional residue of the *Oedipus complex*. The youngest sibling's position, then, is one of vulnerability turned triumphant. Initially weaker, belittled, or bullied, the youngest sibling journeys through inferiority towards recognition, admiration, and hatred.

The hidden warning of this card lies precisely in the cost of the younger sibling's triumph: every victory invites hidden envy. This darkness is not only found externally, but internally as well – for the youngest sibling may feel unconscious guilt about having surpassed their older brothers and sisters, or may feel discomfort regarding the suppressed aggression that arises upon having triumphed over them.

This card reveals themes of sibling rivalry, narcissistic defences, hidden sexual anxieties, unconscious guilt, envy, and competition in the client. Yet the positive aspects of achievement and personal success cannot be ignored either.

SEVEN OF WANDS

In the *Lord of Valour*, we see a young man who holds up a wand in a defensive position against what one would assume to be an unseen assailant, positioned behind the viewer's perspective. His footing is unstable, and his expression suggests that he is aware of his own instability, yet he pushes onward. This card thus represents resistance, defensiveness, and the struggle for dominance. It is a depiction of psychic self-preservation.

Here, the ego, having gained victory, now faces resistance, hostility, opposition, and envy from rivals and/or internal anxieties. The card portrays the ego maintaining its identity and boundaries in the face of internal or external threats. The figure stands upon elevated ground; sequentially, this may symbolically acknowledge the height attained in the *Six*, but the struggle connotes the ego's attempt to maintain moral or psychological dominance, either over internal or external forces.

The wands below, which give both an offensive and defensive impression, symbolise repressed aggression and threats, either from within or without, for one cannot discern whether these wands are directed towards the man or away from him. He is attempting to manage his anxieties, fears, and vulnerabilities through assertiveness and aggression. The isolated background suggests that he will not win this war except through much tribulation.

This image emerges when clients experience psychological defensiveness, internal or external threats to cohesion, aggressive impulses, or emotional isolation. It emphasises the exploration of defence mechanisms, unresolved aggression, persecutory anxiety, and reconciliation with rivals, either internally or literally.

EIGHT OF WANDS

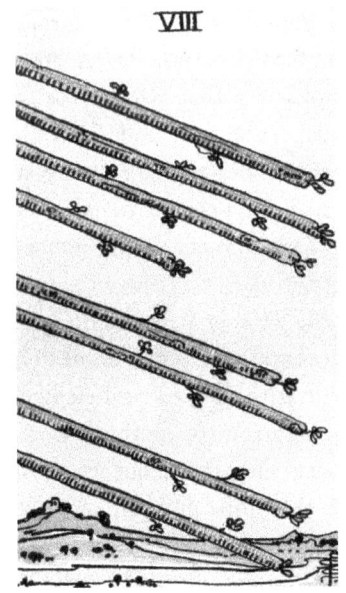

The *Lord of Swiftness*, both in name and in image, is a depiction of movement, breakthrough, and expression. After the resistance and defensiveness of the previous cards, the *Eight* portrays a state of psychological openness where the libido flows unobstructed. The ego, no longer being in a state of paranoiac defensiveness (or so we believe), is now able to allow its emotional and instinctual energies to flow freely toward resolution and satisfaction.

This image illustrates the powerful release of repressed impulses, sexual energy, or emotional desires that were once repressed or inhibited. The wands, as ejecting phallic symbols, recall ejaculation. They fly across the air, as in dreams, suggestive of erection (Freud, 1900). The wands are aligned in flight, indicating that this is not a turbulent expression but a cathartic and harmonious one. The open landscape corroborates this, as it implies a state of emotional freedom and unrestrained manifestation.

This card is the only card of the Tarot, apart from the *Three of Swords*, that does not depict any human figures. Again, this emphasises that what is being dealt with is purely instinctual, energetic, and from the unconscious. Both the *Lord of Sorrow* and *Swiftness* are stripped of their identificatory qualities because there is no subject upon which to identify and project. What remains is the symbol only.

Thus, both the *Three of Swords* and *Eight of Wands* depict pure symbolic events or psychic states. These images are absent of any narrative or theatrical element. There are no protagonists or antagonists in these cards, yet they are indeed assimilated into the sequence of their respective suits. They are therefore pure affective moments in the evolution of the individual.

This image represents breakthroughs, sudden insights, and the expulsion of anxieties and tension. It is an indicator of emotional liberation and movement toward freedom of expression and emotional openness. It may also signal a transition into a new phase of life.

NINE OF WANDS

The *Lord of Great Strength* depicts a man who has surrounded himself with a fortalice of eight wands and clutches fearfully at a ninth. He is bandaged and seemingly injured. His hair is ruffled and his expression is one of caution. In the *Nine of Wands*, we see a depiction of psychic vigilance, defensiveness, and guarded vulnerability. Despite it all, we sense a remnant of perseverance and hope.

It portrays the moment when the ego, having endured struggles, traumas, and tribulations, becomes hypervigilant, defensive, guarded, and emotionally cautious. The man has undergone past traumas and psychic wounds that have cultivated his cautious perseverance. His stance is one of vigilance as he looks beyond the wall of eight wands, representing the symptom of hypervigilance after trauma as a defence against the repetition of the event.

This card conveys the premise that an injured person, no matter how defensive they may be, is still more vulnerable than one who has recovered. It expresses the importance of healing and overcoming trauma rather than building "walls of wands" around oneself. After psychically injurious events, the individual becomes more anxious, sensitive, and insecure. They tend to withdraw and distance themselves psychologically from objects they perceive as threatening or capable of harm.

The emotional fatigue and exhaustion experienced after relational disappointments is expressed in his languid posture, as if on the verge of surrender. Indeed, the figure portrayed herein shall require, as the name suggests, great strength to proceed. It is unclear whether the ninth wand is a weapon, a support, or a burden, although the meaning of this card suggests that it is all three.

The therapeutic implications of this card relate to a client who is on the path of trauma resolution and healing from prolonged anxiety, defensiveness, and guardedness. Clients who identify with this image may benefit from work directed toward rebuilding the capacity for relational trust and emotional openness.

TEN OF WANDS

The *Ten of Wands* is called, in the tradition of the Golden Dawn, the *Lord of Oppression*. We do indeed behold an oppressed figure who carries ten burdensome wands upon his shoulder, seemingly in shame and tribulation. Despite these, there is an estate in the relative distance toward which he is headed. Though it is not visible to him, it remains in sight if he were, hypothetically, to look upwards. This implies that the labour he is undergoing shall eventually come to an end, though not without first having endured the tribulation itself. He must be oppressed before he gains relief.

The *Ten of Wands* depicts a state of ego oppression. This oppression emanates from multiple sources, as implied by the many wands. One of these sources is, of course, the demands of the superego. One can almost hear the voice of the man in the image saying, "I must." This burden seems not to be entirely external but rather self-imposed. The figure has chosen to carry all ten wands at once, thereby reflecting a self-imposed hardship. There is desire present, but no pleasure. Suffering is thus undergone in order to expiate guilt.

One may naturally wonder why the suit of *Wands* ends in such a bleak manner when compared with the optimism of the former cards. When observing the pips sequentially, we see a progression from the ignition of desire to its interaction with others, and finally to the end result of one-sided development. The pips of *Wands* are therefore a cautionary tale about the burden of desire, namely what transpires when desire transforms into obligation.

In therapeutic work, themes concerning labour, work, remorse, regret, and burdens are naturally best addressed when this card emerges. Self-imposed punishments are also relevant. The client who identifies with this image must be encouraged to transform personal pursuits into pleasure rather than sacrificial obligation.

PAGE OF WANDS
OR THE PRINCESS OF THE SHINING FLAME

In *The Rose of the Palace of Fire*, we behold a young page arrayed in a garment of salamanders, adoring a wand. He stands amidst a desert, before three pyramids. I have discussed this image elsewhere in my book, though the meaning of this image shall certainly be obvious to the reader who has made it thus far.

He is the young boy or young adolescent who has discovered his penis and has begun to awaken to his sexual energy. There is no shame, only awe. The landscape is barren because the erotic for him has just begun. He smiles at the upright wand, for it is erect, potent, and unburdened. This is an auto-erotic, masturbatory image. He has attained awareness of sexuality and has awoken to its desire, despite his lack of expertise and novelty.

In the family constellation, this card represents the enthusiastic daughter who is exploring her individual desires. She is learning how to express herself and is coming into awareness of her personal identity. She has begun to experiment with the boundaries of her parents, as well as with the sexual curiosity of her adolescence.

Therapeutically, this *Page of Wands* may indicate a client entering a new phase of desire, creativity, or personal exploration. It may also be beneficial to address narcissistic vulnerabilities that may lie beneath display or bravado.

KNIGHT OF WANDS

In *The Prince of Fire*, we see a young man riding through the same scene as *The Page* on his fiery horse. His helm and suit are ablaze, and he bears a wand in his hand. He is arrayed in salamanders, and he looks confidently beyond.

It is clear that this is a representation of the adolescent libido in full motion. He is no longer in a state of passive curiosity, but rather of venture. He proceeds onward to his sexual conquests and actively pursues sex. He flirts, seduces, and initiates sexual activities. He is imbued with the phallic narcissism of a virile adolescent and navigates the interpersonal dynamics of sexual conquest with confidence. The libido is not only in active pursuit of the sexual object, but also of personal ambitions and creative projects as well. The landscape is not one of barrenness or inexperience, but rather of novel and exotic experiences waiting to be had. He is ambitious and seeks to prove himself equal to, or surpassing, his father.

The Knight of Wands may signal the need to temper instinctual drives with greater foresight and reflection. In many stories, desire leads to the ruin of a young man or woman. Themes regarding sexual assertiveness and performance may also be appropriately explored. Caution regarding impulsivity may likewise be advised.

QUEEN OF WANDS

In *The Queen of Wands*, we see a woman holding a wand in her right hand and a sunflower in her left. Her throne is adorned with lions, and behind her lies the familiar scene of the three pyramids.

The Queen of Wands, as mentioned elsewhere, represents the phallic mother. She bears dual phallic symbols, the wand and the sunflower. Not only is she all-powerful, but she is also desired and fascinating. She, naturally, represents feminine authority. She does not derive her power from the King; rather, she integrates both principles of activity and receptivity equally. The sunflower suggests that she can give affection without diminishing her authority.

If the client is a woman, it is likely that the attainment of personal independence is important for her. If the client is a man, this image may reflect anxiety regarding female sexuality, possibly insecurities concerning sex.

KING OF WANDS

In *The King of the Spirits of Fire*, we see a man enthroned with a flaming crown upon a throne of salamanders. By his side is the symbol of his kingdom, and his cape is adorned with the same. He bears a wand in his right hand and looks over his desert kingdom.

The Lord of the Flame and Lightning represents the phallic father who is imbued with idealised masculinity, strength, and assertiveness. He holds his wand securely, not needing to brandish his power and authority, for it is already established. He differs from the *King of Swords* in that he is not punishing; rather, he serves as a sexual model for the son. He has control over his desires, thus symbolising a strong, integrated ego that successfully directs the libido without being dominated by it.

This card implies that the client has achieved a sense of inner authority and no longer feels the need to overcompensate. The negative polarity of this card is precisely the opposite, and may indicate an inability to assume mature responsibilities. It may also indicate the integration of phallic power. If this card is negatively related, it may indicate narcissistic grandiosity, phallic narcissism, or the need to dominate.

ACE OF PENTACLES

Hence, we arrive at the final suit of the minor arcana, the *Pentacles*. As is standard across the Aces, we witness an emergence from the unconscious into conscious awareness.

In this particular manifestation, the *Root of the Powers of Earth* depicts the emergence of physical awareness, resources, and the bodily self. It must be noted that this image is less turbulent and more gentle than the rest of the Aces. Yet, no matter how gentle the emergence from the unconscious may be, anxiety is certain to follow.

In the Aces, we do not see a full bodily figure emerge from the clouds, only a hand. This recalls the experience of the infant with the maternal object in parts rather than as a whole. Therefore, this hand that gives the pentacle may be a good and nurturing hand that gives gently, or a bad, powerful hand that is threatening in the fact that it comes from beyond the realm of the ego. The enclosed garden of lilies beneath it evokes an Edenic environment, or a womb-like space. Past the archway, however, one sees the mountain in the distance, protruding out of the earth. What lies ahead, beyond the domain of the mother, is the experience and realm of the father.

The symbolic associations between money, faeces, gold, and the anal stage have been exposited by Freud (1959) and by myself in this book. Therefore, for the sake of efficiency, I shall forgo an exposition on it here. Because the Aces are regarded as the foundation of the element they represent, and the suit of *Pentacles* is so closely tied to anality, we can draw our symbolic interpretations from thence. The *Ace of Pentacles* represents the debut of the anal stage.

Freud equated the act of infantile defecation with the act of gift-giving, in which the child produces an abdominal 'gift' from within himself and delivers it to his parents, who tenderly receive it, tend to him, and affectionately tidy him after receiving it. Besides the sentimental pleasure afforded to the child, sexual pleasure is also experienced via the stimulation of the anus. Where once the mother offered her breast milk as a source of pleasure for the child (and herself, naturally), the child now offers his faeces as a source of pleasure for himself and for his caregiver, whom he presumes delights in attending to him as much as he does. Whether this delight is truly mutual (for there are certainly very affectionate parents who do indeed delight in this ritual) is inconsequential to this interpretation.

The child is no longer in a state of passive receptivity but is now in a state of active giving. Thus, the *Ace of Pentacles* represents this very act of offering stool to the caregiver. The gesture of the hand indicates that this is best understood as a gesture of kind giving.

This card can signify either the positive or negative aspects of anality. This refers to either the maturation of drive management or qualities such as hoarding, compulsivity, cleanliness, and so forth. It may also represent a budding sensation of autonomy. The suit of *Pentacles* pertains to the element of earth, physicality, and materiality. Thus, the *Ace* may signal the bodily ego entering into awareness.

TWO OF PENTACLES

In the *Lord of Harmonious Change*, we see a youthful juggler who balances two pentacles in motion, enfolded within an infinity sign. Behind him are turbulent waves and ships. His gaze suggests concentration and deliberate mental effort.

We are entrenched in an image of instability and precariousness. The balancing act, though playful as it may appear, personifies the anal conflict between retaining control (holding onto and conserving faeces) and the urge to release (let go, defecate). The act of juggling itself is a process of retaining and releasing; therefore, the anal child, in this image, oscillates between retaining and expelling their excrement. There is a push–pull dynamic between anal retention and anal expulsion. The task of the juggler (child) is to give each its due without succumbing wholly to either one.

Separate from the anal interpretations, the juggler recalls the ego balancing the demands of the superego and the id amidst the external world (ships, sea). The sea lies behind him, and he seems unaware of its turbulence. Considering the landscape as a projection of the juggler's mind, he is focused on maintaining order lest the anxieties that underlie consume him.

Regarding the two round pentacles as testicles, with the infinity symbol as the scrotal sac, we might interpret the juggler as anxiously protecting and managing his virility. He is in a position where he faces castration anxiety, and he must be able to project control, hence his apparent graciousness.

The *Two of Pentacles*, ultimately, portrays an act of balancing. This card, therefore, signals that the ego is actively engaged in the work of balancing drives. The client is experiencing inner tension (as indicated by the waves) and is consciously trying to manage it. Naturally, meticulous management of finances, schedules, and relationships may arise, followed by bursts of productivity and spending.

If the client relates to the two pentacles as testicles, anxiety regarding masculinity is evident.

THREE OF PENTACLES

The *Lord of Material Works* presents us with an image of a monk, a mason, and an architect building a cathedral together. As with the other Threes and their relationship to triangulation, I shall preserve the relationship between this card and the former until the conclusive remarks of the Minor Arcana. The young mason's labour with a hammer and chisel is an image of sublimation. Anal impulses (the urge to dominate and to create order) are being sublimated into craftsmanship and the grandiosity of the construction.

The psyche has recognised multiple others, their distinct roles, and their impact upon the external world together with the self. The mason evokes the role of the young child who perceives the presence of the mother and father, seeking their approval. The act of constructing the cathedral creates a container for the mason's individual drives and emotions, akin to a holding environment. The supportive presence of two figures at his right absorbs his anal anxiety and aggression, transforming them into creativity and collaboration.

What intrigues me most about this card is that it is the only image in the entire Minor Arcana that does not feature the emblem of the suit. There are no coins whatsoever in this image. The figures behold a column upon which we see the white rose of York and the engraving of the pentacles, but not the pentacles themselves. The content of the libido has been sublimated into a socially acceptable and creative form. It is, therefore, the erotic in disguise. Alternatively, it may also signal the very act of sublimation itself. The anal drive (pentacle) has been sublimated and transformed into a creative statue.

The image of the *Three of Pentacles* invites the viewer to question how they are utilising their impulses, and whether they are cooperating with or envying others in their lives. Themes of creativity and collaboration are evident. Sublimation as a defence is clear as well.

FOUR OF PENTACLES

The title *Lord of Earthly Power* gives us a considerable amount of insight into the psychology of this personage, whom we behold clutching anxiously onto one pentacle, with two at his feet and one upon his crown. 'Earthly power' is a precarious thing, for, as we see behind him what one can suppose to be his realm, it can at once be easily lost. Earthly power does indeed afford riches and authority, but once one is left without it, one is nothing.

The lord lacks an extravagant throne or flamboyant dress, both typical of one of his class. He wears the pentacle upon his simple crown as a grandiose compensation for his modesty. He rests his feet upon the two pentacles awkwardly, as if both giving them purpose and protecting them. The star at the centre of his body is held with utmost care. He very clearly holds onto his 'earthly power' with paranoia, defensiveness, and anxiety. His posture is tense and speaks to a need for control, which is the price of earthly power.

I shall keep the anal correspondences of this image brief, since this card is an aspect of the psychosexual sequence of the Tarot which has already been much exposited. I shall, therefore, keep what I have to say regarding such matters in connection with it concise. The *Four of Pentacles* very aptly portrays the image of the anal character, who rigidly organises his world and keeps his treasures safe. He is the child who gains security and self-mastery by "holding everything in." It is for this reason that I have identified the card as the anal-retentive character.

An interesting aspect of this card is that the figure is in a state of solitude. He is entirely detached from the town in the background. Additionally, the greedy overtones of this card are apparent. Greed is naturally associated with narcissism, for beneath greed lies the unconscious desire to incite it within others. Thus, there is a narcissistic element underlying this card. When combining his isolation, defensiveness, and narcissism into one, we find what Hyman Spotnitz (1962; 1976) called "narcissistic insulation". This is a self-defensive method wherein one keeps others at bay so that no one can intrude upon or injure them. This isolation, naturally, comes at the psychological cost of loneliness. While this stance psychologically provides him with a sense of safety and autonomy, it imprisons him in a state of tension and separateness. We then witness a clear dilemma: the more one guards, the more one loses.

As much as it relates to anal matters, it also suggests a fear of letting go, a fear of vulnerability, and an attachment to earthly goods. The coin that he clutches at his heart symbolises emotional guardedness. He has symbolically plated his heart with armour against intimacy. The *Lord of Earthly Power* has chosen love of money over love of another, for the latter is far more costly than the former. His crown is a clear narcissistic façade. The two pentacles beneath his feet indicate that the foundation of his internal world is built upon obsessive security. They also call to mind the potty training of infants, who use footstools to support themselves. In therapy, this card may also signal withholding on the part of the reticent client who is reluctant to "give" his emotions to the therapist. Compensatory narcissism is a clear theme as well.

FIVE OF PENTACLES

We witness a rather lamentable and bleak scene when beholding the *Lord of Material Trouble*. The *Five of Pentacles* depicts two beggars, one of them leprous, walking miserably through snow-covered land. Behind and above them is a stained-glass window containing five pentacles.

It is worth noting that these pitiable figures are beyond the walls of a cathedral, perhaps even the very same cathedral of the *Three of Pentacles*. In the *Three*, we saw the cathedral as a work in progress, whereas in the *Five*, we see it (implicitly) perfected. This mirrors the experience of one who once had security and belonging but now suffers the loss of an internal or external resource, an experience of loss accompanied by shame.

Shame is an anal emotion, for being dirty with faeces is equated with feelings of being shameful. This emotion is powerfully expressed by the *Five of Pentacles*, most especially in the dirtiness of the figures, particularly in the case of the leper. They are bereft of earthly goods and now roam the land in remorseful abandon. The figures in the *Five* carry deep narcissistic wounds and are thus psychically injured. We see the man bandaged and crippled, and the woman fares no better. It is as if the *Five* indicates the fate that awaits the lord of the *Four*.

Therapeutically, it is essential to explore feelings of helplessness and shame when working with this image. The client may feel deficient or inadequate in relation to the external world. Experiences of neglect are also appropriate to explore. This is not a very positive card, so optimistic alternatives are difficult to conjure. This is a card of lack, self-punishment, and loss.

SIX OF PENTACLES

As with other cards that appear in my psychosexual sequence, I shall keep my connection between the *Lord of Material Success* and anal expulsivity brief. In this more optimistic image, we see a handsome lord giving coins to a beggar. In his left hand, he holds a scale above another beggar. Above him, overshadowing him, hang six pentacles.

His smile, and the gaze of hope with which the two beggars look upon him, give a sense that success is meant to be shared. This image is therefore one of generosity and release, the latter indicated by his release of four coins. It is as if, by releasing the four coins, he undoes or opposes the stance of the *Four of Pentacles*. He reflects the shift from defensive retention to generous release.

To keep my exposition on this image brief, this card emphasises not only the need to share one's gifts with the world, but also to be open and receptive to it as well. A common shadow of the suit of Pentacles is the enclosure of oneself socially or interpersonally. Therefore, the *Six of Pentacles* encourages openness with others.

SEVEN OF PENTACLES

The image of the *Lord of Success Unfulfilled* is a rather complex one. At first glance, one gets the sense that it represents hard work and the harvest thereof, but this is an oversimplification when both the name and the expression of the farmer are considered. The man beholds his crop of six pentacles, with a seventh fallen near his foot, beside his hoe. He rests upon it and gazes over his harvest with an expression of discontent.

One initially gets the sense that the message of the card is to pause and contemplate one's accumulated treasure. His expression, however, reveals that there is much more than meets the eye. He has reaped a poor harvest and now laments his condition. It seems as though he hesitates even to reap the crop, for in doing so he must part with it. It is this exact moment of pause which, I believe, strikes the viewer most upon first observing this card.

The ability to wait and delay gratification is a sign of maturity. He is able to delay the energy of his id (reaping) until it can be released (harvested) at a more suitable time and place. This is the child who has developed a tolerance for frustration and is able to postpone the experience of pleasure and the discharge of tension.

We also get a sense of what the time before this very moment must have looked like, for the farmer likely began his venture with grandiose hopes. He likely imagined a much more abundant harvest than the one he was truly met with. He is thus experiencing a narcissistic deflation as the principle of reality asserts itself upon him. This has caused him fatigue, as conveyed by his stance.

When an individual feels the loss of something valued (esteem, time, effort), anger is often turned inward, producing a unique state of depression. His countenance reflects this precise condition. He has become aware of the gap between his effort and the outcome, likely leading to guilt as well. His anxiety over his crop is tied to his sense of personal competence, as though the failure of the crop indicated personal failure too. This, in turn, leads him to feel that he has been "bad" or "lazy", reinforcing the development of psychological fatigue. His fatigue is therefore a by-product of the feelings incited by his disillusion.

In the therapeutic context, the *Seven of Pentacles* reflects a client's ambivalence regarding their achievements, and whether they are "good enough". Sequentially, we see moments of highs and lows throughout the suit of Pentacles, perhaps alluding to the fact that, in life, one's economy is hardly ever a straight and narrow movement upward. It is more akin to a series of rises and falls which, with effort, purpose, and persistence, incline upward.

EIGHT OF PENTACLES

The *Lord of Material Prudence* offers a rather straightforward meaning to the viewer. In it, we see a craftsman forging a pentacle with his hammer and chisel. Six pentacles are hung upon the wall, and the eighth lies at his feet. We get the sense that he is in his workshop, and we see a path leading from his place of work to the town behind him.

This scene once again symbolises the sublimation of the anal drive. Parallel to the *Three*, the anal urge to control, soil, and retain has been sublimated into creativity and purposeful work. Whereas the *Three* portrayed this in a social manner, the *Eight* portrays it as an individual process. Following the disappointment experienced in the previous card, the ego has not given up; it has reinvested its energy into productivity, mastery, and skill. Here, the ego has developed enough to renounce immediate or grandiose gratification and has learned the value of toiling through accumulated skill. The satisfaction here is not only delayed but also internal.

The orderliness of the anal personality is reflected in the six aligned pentacles along the wall. Individuals who repetitively dream of or draw vertical structures are often working through themes of control and aspiration. Likewise, Freud (1955; 1959) observed that the play of children who enjoy repetitively stacking and knocking down blocks echoes controlled anal retention and subsequent release. Thus, the stacked pentacles reflect the internal sense of control and the unconscious ambitions of the craftsman, now being perfected in a mature and realistic manner.

The *Eight of Pentacles* yields insights related to work, control, perfectionism, self-imposed high standards, delayed gratification, reparation, and defences against chaos. It also relates to ambition, confidence, and the formation of identity. Underlying all of these, however, is the achievement of self-satisfaction.

NINE OF PENTACLES

The *Lord of Material Gain* is one of the most fortunate cards in the entire Tarot. In this image, we behold a woman of noble standing luxuriating in a vineyard, arrayed in a floral garment styled in accordance with the symbol of Venus. Around her and among the vines are nine pentacles, one of which she comfortably rests her arm upon. On her other hand is perched a falcon, and behind her stands her estate. Above the scene stretches a golden sky.

The woman of the *Nine of Pentacles*, confidently alone in her vineyard, has not only attained material mastery but also mastery over the anal drive. Her external environment is flourishing because she has mastered her internal one. The pentacles that surround her are the sublimated fruits of anal achievement, wealth gained through discipline.

Her posture exudes solemnity, indicating self-sufficiency. Her mastery of the bird may also symbolise the sublimation of primitive drives.

The erotic-narcissistic tones of this card are ostensible. We can see that she is narcissistically cathected. Her libidinal energy has been withdrawn from others and returned to her ego and its extensions (her garden, fruits, wealth, and so forth). On one hand, she exudes self-reliance and autonomy, yet on the other, we perceive a defensive "all I need is myself" attitude, the latter being a defence against dependency, loss, and disappointment.

Her dignity and austere countenance could be interpreted as the ego gazing upon itself as a love object, like Narcissus in the river. In the psychoanalysis of narcissism, the libido becomes attached to the ego, and the ego becomes its own erotic focus. Her garment, arrayed with the symbols of Venus, and her luxuriation among the treasures with which she surrounds herself, create a world in which she is the central treasure. Even her estate, seen in the background, is not the central focus; rather, she is.

The hidden warning of this image, as is present in all the images of the Tarot, may be the presence of erotic narcissism: the libidinal gratification obtained through self-love.

Her costume has been chosen out of exhibitionism. The opulence of her garden and the nine pentacles are laid out for the onlooker's gaze. Her slight smile and her poise suggest an awareness, albeit subtle, of being seen as an object of admiration, greed, and envy. Even the falcon, which at first glance may seem a romantic device within the painting, in fact holds meaning. Falconry was historically a privilege of nobility, so her mastery of the bird advertises her elite position. Every element of her presentation has therefore been curated to affirm her sense of self-value.

This card may indicate, in addition to the aforementioned, an ego that has fortified itself. Positively, there is a sense of completeness that accompanies this card. Themes of healthy self-love and narcissistic self-sufficiency are appropriate to bring up when this card is identified with.

TEN OF PENTACLES

The *Ten of Pentacles* provides an encouraging end to the pips of Pentacles. Following the disappointment of the *Seven*, we see the continued effort, or prudence, of the *Eight*, the material reward of perseverance in the *Nine*, and now the long-term reward of the *Ten*. It is as if the suit itself were to inspire one to persevere and refine oneself, however many failures there may be, for each failure is truly a step closer to success and lasting satisfaction.

It is perhaps for this reason that it is called the *Lord of Wealth*. The very word *wealth* differs greatly from *abundance* or *gain*, for *wealth* implies the acquisition not only of valuable goods but also of resources, assets, possessions, and objects of worth that distinguish and elevate a family socially. Wealth carries with it a sense of security, opportunity, legacy, and family, whereas *gain* or *goods* do not. The riches acquired in the *Nine* may very well be lost by a frivolous or vain possessor, but the *Ten* indicates judicious and prudent management of what was gained and earned.

Symbolically, thrift, orderliness, stubbornness, parsimony, and all the conflicts of anality have been triumphed over. In the context of the lifespan, the difficult lessons of productive mastery and autonomy have now been consolidated into established wealth and stability. This card denotes the closure of the lessons of the anal stage.

In this image, we see an elderly man clothed in elegant robes, sitting beside two dogs. Ten golden pentacles are arranged across the image in the form of a tree. Before him stands what we may assume to be his family, and upon the wall behind them is his crest. This is an intergenerational depiction, for we can assume that we see at least one of his children and his grandchildren.

The young couple, or siblings, before him stand in the archway of his palace with their son or nephew, indicating to the viewer that they are about to inherit his legacy, not only his material inheritance. The crests upon the wall also corroborate this. We therefore witness the lineage of the superego successfully handed from the patriarch to his descendants.

It should be clear that this image, in therapy, brings up themes of lineage, legacy, and symbolic immortality. By curating a legacy, a home, a coat of arms, and wealth, the patriarch hopes to transcend death. By leaving a legacy, he has pacified his anxiety about dying by assuring himself that he shall "live on." The negative aspect of this card may indicate a need for control over, or preoccupation with, the future. Anxiety regarding ageing and succession is also appropriately applied.

PAGE OF PENTACLES
OR PRINCESS OF ECHOING HILLS

The *Rose of the Palace of Earth* introduces us to the family of stability and practicality. In this image, we see a young knave holding a pentacle in his hand with great respect and adoration. Before him lies a flourishing, abundant land. Above him stretches a golden sky.

The *Page of Pentacles* gazes intently at the star in his hands, like the adolescent who has discovered his own body. The erotic here is investigative and invites experimentation. This is the adolescent whose sexual awakening has been activated through observation and reverie. He gazes upon the pentacle as if asking, "What is this? What can I do with it?"—echoing his own feelings about his genitals.

In this image, we see the daughter of the royal family of Pentacles, who is at the very beginning of her journey towards autonomy. She may have begun to assert herself and may have experienced a few errors, but the fertile and edenic land before her indicates that she is safe to make mistakes and capable of recovering from them. She has just become aware of her bodily autonomy and has begun to receive the familial transmission of practical knowledge and skills necessary for her navigation of the adult world. She now enters the era of mature reality testing.

This card may naturally expose a vulnerability to perfectionism and naïvety. Themes of growth, maturation, and adulthood saturate the card.

KNIGHT OF PENTACLES

The *Prince of the Chariot of Earth* depicts a young, heavily armoured man who sits upon a black horse, holding a pentacle in his hand and overlooking a ploughed, fertile land. The golden sky canopies the field.

There comes a moment in the development of sexuality in the young boy that is inundated with fear. The adolescent becomes frightened by the strength of his sexual fantasies and urges. He is afraid that they may, and often do, overcome his physical body, as in the case of unwanted erections and nocturnal emissions. Within the royal family of Pentacles, we see a lineage that has mastered both its internal and external reality. The adolescent knight has learned self-control amidst the navigation of his sexuality and the independence that accompanies puberty.

The *Knight* has identified with the supportive father and has internalised, or begun to internalise, the lessons of perseverance. He wishes to be seen as the "good son" and worthy of parental respect. In contrast to the *Knight of Swords*, he remains obedient to his parents. The suit of Pentacles, in fact, stands in opposition to the Swords (Mathers & Felkin, 1890s/ n.d.). Hence, he seeks independence not through rebellion, but through approval.

This card may be interpreted therapeutically as similar to the *Page of Pentacles*, with the distinction that it implies being stationary when one needs to be in motion. The client must take care that their self-worth is not intrinsically tied to their achievements or the fulfilment of family values. His complete stillness may indicate a creative or seminal inhibition, for he may, in the negative sense, hold in his creative or sexual output out of fear of its shameful implications. His diligent posture may then serve as a defensive position against performance anxiety. Beneath the surface, we see a tension between family and self. Within, there is a strong possibility of a swirl of unexpressed emotions that are cautiously reined.

QUEEN OF PENTACLES

The *Queen of the Thrones of Earth* depicts a gentle woman enthroned upon a seat adorned with angels and fruit. Upon her head rests a golden rooster, and around her are fruits and flowers. A rabbit leaps nearby, and a golden sky envelops her land. She cradles a pentacle upon her lap.

Motherhood and fertility abound in this image. Everything, from the symbols to the environment and even her gaze, radiates maternity. By viewing this image, we are immersed in the realm of the mother. The way she holds and adores the pentacle resembles a mother holding her child or infant. The *Queen of Pentacles* is a safe and secure container for her children's affect. She is affectionate and loving without infantilising. I do not have much more to say regarding this image, except that it is the picture of the good internal mother.

KING OF PENTACLES

The *Lord of the Wide and Fertile Land*, *King of the Spirits of the Earth*, brings us to the end of my analysis of the suit of Pentacles, as well as that of the Minor Arcana. In this image, we see the handsomely gowned King of Earth seated upon the throne of his castle, which bears four extravagant engravings of Taurus, the bull. Upon his head rests a beautiful crown of golden flowers, and his robe is adorned with grapes, resembling the vineyard of the *Lady of Material Gain*. Grapes abound around him. He rests his arm upon a pentacle, and in his right hand he holds a sceptre. Above his castle stretches a golden sky.

The portrait of the *King of Pentacles* is the image that the *Knight of Pentacles* aspires to emulate and please. His environment shows that he is merciful, though his face conveys a certain severity. His negative aspect is that he may replace presence with provision and equate love with economic support. Nevertheless, he is the father who knows both how to frustrate pleasure and how to gratify it.

The hidden warning of this card lies in the armoured foot that emerges from his robes. This may indicate that he is highly sexual in potential but either appears to, or actually does, restrain his appetite. The armoured foot suggests that narcissistic precautions are still in place. There remains an aspect of himself that cannot allow him to fully relax.

The cardinal message of this image, in therapy, is that in order to master the external world, one must first master the internal world. The external world is a mirror and responds to the internal; therefore, if the client seeks to change their living circumstances, they must first change their internal environment.

CLOSING STATEMENT
REGARDING THE SUITS

The *Minor Arcana*, as I have exhaustively exposited, refer to events, passages, experiences, and stages of life, each bearing its own positives, negatives, and warnings. It is clear that each client will relate to the *Minor Arcana* differently, and that a single, fixed interpretation would result in failure. Clients will perceive each card as either threatening or inviting in accordance with their own internal environment.

I have spoken extensively about the significance of the number three in psychology. The Tarot, as a reflection of the psyche, likewise illustrates the importance of this number. If we look at the four Threes, Wands, Cups, Swords, and Pentacles, we find a distinct narrative and depiction of triangulation.

Beginning with the Wands, we see a solitary figure gazing toward the sea and framed by three wands. Two stand behind him, and one is grasped. This represents the triangulation of ego, desire, and the external world. This card reflects the symbolic third, the Name-of-the-Father, who interrupts the dyad of infant and mother. He does not paralyse the child, however; he introduces the child to the realm of possibility, social order, independence, and the future. He impels the child away from his home as a force that urges him forward.

The man in the *Three of Wands* stands with two wands behind him while holding his own. He is no longer engulfed in fusion and is now able to desire something else. In this image, triangulation is connected to the future, to planning, separation, and goal-directed individuation. The number three in this card signifies separation and individuation, reminiscent of the entrance into adulthood.

In the *Three of Cups*, we see the ego, the ideal ego, and the social other engaged in an image of harmony. Each of the Graces is an echo of the other, distinct yet very similar. Here we see an image of the ego, represented by the central figure, reflected in the company of the ideal and the social other. There is a mirroring and identification that takes place within this card. Desire circulates through the gaze and the recognition of the ideal and the other. Each of the figures finds themselves in one another.

This is an image of triangulation on the social level, wherein the ego is developed and structured through the participation of the psyche in social interaction and the external world. The concealed face, however, may suggest the risk of betrayal, disharmony, and competition. Nevertheless, this card depicts the social aspect of the number three.

The *Three of Swords* presents the bleakest form of triangulation in the shape of betrayal, pain, and heartbreak. It is one of the only images in the entire Tarot (the other being the *Eight of Wands*) that contains no human or animal figures. It is a direct and undiluted image of pain. This represents the moment when the subject is excluded from the nuclear dyad, when they are no longer the sole object of the mother's or father's love. In mature relationships, it depicts the experience of discovering that one's beloved has offered their heart to another.

In this card, the number three signifies wounding. It is not celebratory, as in the *Cups*, nor generative, as in the *Wands*. The three pierced swords represent attachment, love, and loss. The number three in this card conveys exclusion from the intimate two.

Lastly, the *Three of Pentacles* depicts a mason, a monk, and an artisan constructing what appears to be a cathedral. This is a harmonious triangulation in which each distinct person plays a necessary role. It represents the foundational triad of the family: child, mother, and father. Each individual participates in the family system, collaborating within their respective social roles.

The number three in this card represents structure and the sublimated result of Oedipal resolution. Desire is no longer destructive, and the libido is no longer incestuous or rivalrous. It is channelled into work, creativity, and society.

✣ 6 ✣
THE OPERATION OF TAROT PSYCHOLOGY & PSYCHOTHERAPEUTIC IMPLICATIONS

FIGURE 4.0

Psychosexual Sequence of the Tarot

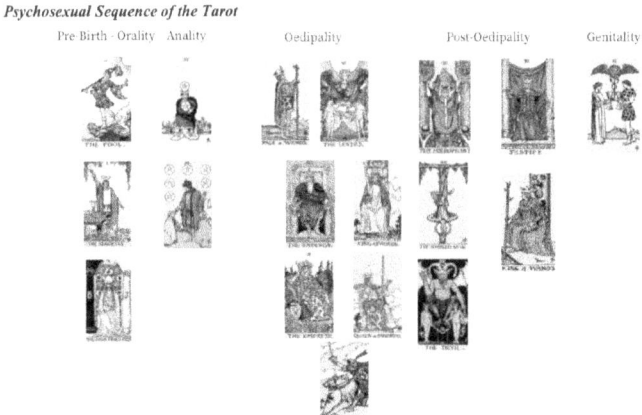

The foundational premise of all psychoanalytic psychotherapy is that the unconscious knows all that consciousness does not. If one cannot accept this (as many cannot), then one cannot accept psychoanalysis at all. The fact remains that there are deep and repressed aspects of the human being that are as dark and minacious as the profundity of the sea. These aspects exist within all individuals, and it is one of the chief tasks of life to venture into the darkness of the earth in order to confront the darkness within oneself and emerge transformed.

Thus, Hercules had to conquer his twelve trials before his ascent to Olympus; Jesus had to descend into the underworld before his glorious resurrection; Psyche had to journey to the underworld before her marriage to Cupid in heaven, and so forth. Recall the countless stories in which heroes confront a mighty dragon before their triumph: St George and the Dragon, St Martha, Mary and the Dragon in the *Apocalypse of St John the Apostle*, Prince Philip in *Sleeping Beauty*, and many others.

The dragon represents the darkness within oneself that must be externalised, confronted, and tamed in order to attain illumination, self-discovery, and inner success. The bliss achieved after conquering the dragon represents the state of satisfaction that follows self-acceptance and understanding. Mythology, resistant to time and age, has long instructed humanity in the ancient truths of life's mysteries. The Tarot, as a mythology of human existence, is no different.

Mythology, within a psychotherapeutic framework, functions through personification. The characters within stories are personifications of human phenomena, character types, and internal parts. By comparison, a person can be likened to a play, while the actors within the play represent the different parts of the self. In mythological and complex psychology, certain characters are more closely identified with than others or are invested with greater psychic energy. The traits, qualities, and typologies of these characters already exist, but the characters themselves give them name and form.

For example, in the case of the *Fortunata Complex* (Barraca Mairal, 2015; de Justin, 2025), we see the profile of a woman who is selflessly and chronically in love with a married man. Although the character Fortunata was created in the nineteenth century, by the time her story was told, the world had already known countless women like her.

As mentioned in my introduction, the Tarot inherently contains meanings both of and within itself. It is unique, however, in that its meanings may also manifest distinctly according to the perception, experience, belief, and internal environment of the individual. Thus, while retaining its own dignity and meaning, the viewer may also project their own definitions onto the cards. For one person, the *Four of Cups* may represent contemplation and meditation; for another, it may symbolise stubborn refusal of assistance or pessimism.

The use of the Tarot in therapy is therefore parallel to the use of projective tests such as the *Thematic Apperception Test*. The Tarot arguably holds an advantage over the TAT in that it is inherently encoded with cultural, psychological, and philosophical symbolism.

Projective tests are called "projective" because they function on the principle of projection, wherein what is internal is treated as though it were external (Freud, 1915). The internal contents of the individual are thus projected onto a receptive or interpretative medium, through which the analyst can interpret and decipher these internal contents. Whatever subject is to be made known to the therapist, the therapist must find an inciting object—one that elicits a reaction from the corresponding domain of the internal world—and observe what is projected outward by the client.

This process is often, at least in part, performed

unknowingly by the ego. Through projection, the ego ensures comfort and wards off discomfort by expelling unpleasant qualities of itself and attributing them to others. Although criticisms may arise regarding the measurement and utilisation of projective tools such as images and graphology, it is precisely these same principles that underpin modern methods such as art therapy and journaling.

In the practice of tarot psychology and psychotherapy, the primary defence mechanism employed is projection. The client projects their internal world onto the image of the card and perceives that image in accordance with their own internal environment.

Figure 5.0

Projective Loop in Tarot Psychotherapy

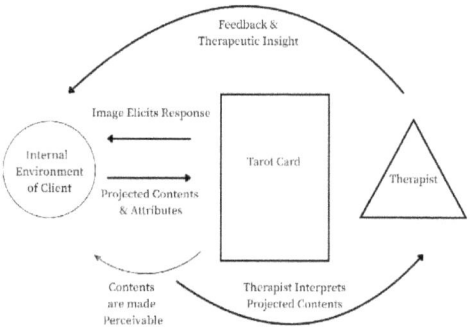

In this table, I demonstrate how the client's internal environment interacts with the projective symbolism of the Tarot. The client is presented with an image that elicits a response from their internal world, based on its inherent symbolism. The client then projects the corresponding contents and attributes onto the card, whereby these are made perceivable. The client, associating the image with what is contained within themselves, verbally characterises the image according to what is being projected. The therapist then receives this verbal feedback, interprets the client's comments, and uses them as insight or clinical material.

The contents drawn forth are observable through the client's narratives, symbolic interpretations, and emotional reactions to the cards. Other defence mechanisms that may be activated include repression, seen especially when a client consistently or adamantly avoids, or is averse to, a particular card. This may explain why images such as *The Devil* or *Death* are often desired to be put away or discarded, as they represent the most difficult and intolerable aspects of the self. One must then ask what is being avoided by the client.

Displacement frequently occurs when an image evokes a memory of a certain place or object, commonly a person or interpersonal situation. Identification may also naturally take place, as the characters of the cards can embody internal objects or psychic parts.

The cards themselves illustrate various mechanisms of defence. Defensive denial is best represented by the *Two of Swords*, she who is blindfolded and refuses to act amidst evident tension. Denial of action is embodied by the *Four of Cups*, the figure seated with crossed arms beneath the tree, seemingly indifferent to the hand that emerges beside him from the cloud. Regression is depicted by the *Six of Cups*, where we see not only a scene of emotional innocence but also a child stooping before a grandmotherly figure. *Temperance*, peacefully situated between devastating images, aptly represents reaction formation, which transforms unacceptable impulses into their opposite. The *Eight of Pentacles* symbolises sublimation, with the craftsman working in diligent focus, having transformed his instincts into a constructive and creative expression.

The *Tarot* images themselves function almost identically to dream symbols – their usage likewise paralleling dream work. Like dream symbols, *Tarot* images condense multiple meanings into one visual form via symbolic condensation. Emotional states, conflicts, desires, fears, aspirations, etc. may all be represented by a single image. *The Tower*, for instance, symbolises collapse, failure, upheaval, repressed rage, and finality – all depending on the client's associations. Freud (1900) pointed out the mechanism of displacement in dreams – paralleling a dream sword with a phallus. In *Tarot*, as established, the same phenomenon occurs. Like dream images, *Tarot* images too are subjective and elastic – their meaning may change with each client or simply over time. *Tarot*, like dream therapy, operates on the logic of the unconscious. It relies on metaphor, emotional truth, symbolism, etc. It is not rational or mathematical.

In dream work, the dreamer narrates the story of the dream. In *Tarot* psychotherapy, the client describes what is going on in the cards, invents a story, etc. The analyst explores symbols and affect tied to both dream and *Tarot* symbols. Free association and inner states disguised by symbol and metaphor also come to the surface in both dream and *Tarot* work. The psychotherapist may ask, "What do you see in this card?" in the same manner he asks, "What does this dream image remind you of?" The client is then encouraged to free associate with the card. The practitioner may ask: "What does this card feel like? If it could speak, what would it tell you? Does it remind you of anyone?"

The images of the *Tarot* draw from the client's personal mythology and give name to what has no name, making conscious what was formerly unconscious. It is for all the aforementioned reasons that the therapist cannot read *Tarot* for a client outside of the therapeutic space, since the function of the cards relies on projection and transference of the client's own internal world onto them.

The images of the *Tarot* may also be used to perform guided active imagination. The therapist may invite the client to engage directly with the images, figures, or voices of the *Tarot* from within the unconscious. In active imagination, the client is guided into a state of profound daydreaming in which they engage with the unconscious. Once there, they allow the image to speak for itself rather than attempt to control it. The client is encouraged to let the symbol express itself, no matter how absurd, irrational, or shameful it may seem.

The *Tarot* cards, inherently, invite self-reflection. Even to the uninformed observer, when beholding the cards they are inclined to ask, "Why is that there? What does it mean?" With seventy-eight images, the *Tarot* provides an abundant wellspring of information to draw from. To do this, the card must first be conceptualised as a portal. Once done, the client is guided to step into the scene of the card, becoming an observer and/or participant within it.

The client then focuses on the image and speaks directly to the figure, either aloud or within the imagination. They then step into the identity of the figure and notice the feelings, emotions, and/or wounds the figure may suffer. From there, they may change the scene, inquire further, heal, or revisit a certain time or moment in their life, having assumed the form of the symbol.

Now that I have demonstrated how the *Tarot* cards function as portals, I believe it is a wonderful moment to exposit how they may be used as hypnotic portals in therapy. The Golden Dawn used the images of the *Tarot* as hypnotic and meditative mediums (Asprem, 2017), so their function as such is already ingrained in their earliest history (and intention).

During hypnotherapy, when the ego's defences are softened, the mind becomes more receptive to symbolic language. The visual richness, symbolic depth, and mythic language of the cards make them perfect tools to incorporate into hypnotherapy. Firstly, the card can be used as an anchoring device. The vividness of its colours and the symbolic abundance of the imagery fixate the eyes and can serve as an induction into hypnosis or as a deepening technique – akin to mirror-gazing or flame-gazing.

The cards may also be used as a projective screen for the hypnotherapist – what the client 'sees' in the card is what needs to be addressed. The card then becomes a bridge between the unconscious and the conscious, one that the therapist can guide the client across. It is encouraged to take the client as deep and profound as possible for this work. I recommend the second (Cataleptic) or third (Somnambulic) level of hypnotic depth for *Tarot* work.

Thus, after performing the appropriate inductions, deepenings, and progressive relaxations, the client is taken into a chosen or petitioned card – incorporating the relevant colours, details, symbols, etc. Because the card contains personified forces or aspects of the self, the hypnotherapist thereby gains access to these parts of the client. The client may also converse with these figures, understand them, and improve their relationship with them.

Clients may be guided to heal, identify, or integrate with the *Tarot* image. The active imagination framework applies particularly well here. The *Tarot* can then be used as a symbolic anchor from which the client may draw. Together, the client and therapist can access unconscious material, reveal and transform inner conflicts and parts, re-script limiting beliefs or past traumas through symbolic enactment, and facilitate integration with the split-off aspects of the self.

The writings of Ouspensky, which I referenced during my analysis of the Major Arcana, are accurate representations of the hypnotic and imaginal journey through the *Tarot*.

To close the chapter, I think it befitting to introduce the method I have personally elaborated. I do not know of any individual who has written about or expounded upon this formula – firstly, because the field of *Tarot* psychology itself remains in its infancy, and secondly, because I am unaware of anyone else who has blended psychology, *Tarot*, and hypnotherapy to create a coherent formula for psychotherapy or other therapeutic practices.

Thus, I shall share my own method, derived from my cumulative research and experience. This framework may, of course, be adapted to suit varying therapeutic needs and preferences.

After introducing the *Tarot* to the client as a symbolic wellspring and a kind of psychological and symbolic dictionary, I do one of two things. If the client specifically requests the use of the *Tarot* or expresses an interest in "seeing how it works", I perform the Celtic Cross spread for them in accordance with the Golden Dawn tradition. As Rosengarten (2000) states, there are various 'styles' of interpreting the fantasy content of the cards.

The *Analytic* style is based on analysis and correspondence; it takes one card at a time and examines its multiple meanings. The *Therapeutic* style is grounded in reflection and perception – the interpreter becomes more supportive, and the goal is self-discovery for the querent. The *Psychic* style is based on intuition and subtle sensory awareness, while the *Magical* style is founded upon positive affirmation and conscious intent.

I then intuit the style most suited to the client. My work with them will usually inform me, or they themselves will indicate what they are seeking – whether it is to 'know more' or to gain 'clarity'. I then proceed through the Celtic Cross spread with them. After doing so, I ask the client which card 'speaks to them the most'. This question reveals the unconscious need that is seeking expression.

I then perform the appropriate inductions and progressive relaxations. Before conducting the staircase deepening, I use an eye-fascination technique, having the client focus on the image of the card until their eyes gently close. Once deepened, I commence the trancework, followed by the count upward, accompanied by the appropriate affirmations. The total operation takes roughly one and a half to two hours, depending on how the therapist works.

The utilisation of synchronicity is plain: synchronicity operates upon the significance of meaningful coincidence. These moments of coincidence offer profound personal and therapeutic insight. In moments of synchronicity, the external and internal worlds mirror one another, producing a symbolic event that passes through resistance or filters. Thus, by casting the Celtic Cross, I employ the principle of synchronicity to bypass denial and the ego's filters – both towards the unconscious and the external world.

Not only does this process affirm what the client may fear, doubt, or intuitively sense, but it also strengthens the therapeutic alliance. The client feels that one has "opened a door for them nobody else has." It further encourages the client to begin thinking symbolically. The *Tarot* cards thus facilitate the emergence of synchronicity. I have termed this method the Imaginal Symbol Induction Technique.

If the client expresses neither an interest nor a disinterest in the *Tarot*, I will, after explaining its significance, show them an image (or images) I believe resonate with them and conduct the appropriate and previously established inquiries. At this stage, hypnosis depends on the client and the course of therapy. Usually, those who come seeking *Tarot*-incorporated methods of therapy are more open to its use than those who do not – which is why, with the latter, I omit the utilisation of the Celtic Cross. This latter method of identification followed by psychological inquiry I have termed The Projective Tarot Method.

What distinguishes the ISIT from the TPTM is that, in the case of the former, the use of an analytic spread followed by hypnosis is involved. In the latter, there is no hypnosis or spread – only symbolic insight followed by explorative inquiry. I shall elaborate upon these methods with much greater profundity in a later work.

In either case, I have never received an oppositional comment from a client, whether prospective or paying, regarding my *Tarot* practice. With honesty (and honour), the only negative remark I have ever received was from a client who, at the end of the third free session with me (which I offered to all prospective clients at the time), told me that he had seen that I "did *Tarot*" and disliked it due to previous negative associations with fortune-tellers and psychics. When I explained my practice of *Tarot*, and that I did not employ it with all clients – much less with clients antagonistic towards it – he then told me that he was not interested in paying for hypnotherapy and that he preferred to spend the remaining money he had each month on marijuana and beer.

I shall commend the reader to discern the foundation of his behaviour and negative statements – though I believe them to be quite evident. This is not to suggest that *Tarot*-related methods are incompatible with, for example, Christian-based beliefs or clients. After all, the *Tarot* is far more Christian in essence than many would initially presume. I once had a client who ascribed to the group of Black Hebrew Israelites, and he held a strong affinity for the *Tarot* and for *Tarot*-related work.

One cannot presume antagonism at the outset, yet neither should one presume compatibility either – though this, most certainly, applies to everything in therapy.

At the heart of every therapeutic practitioner's work with *Tarot* implementation should be their own personal engagement with the *Tarot*. Before using *Tarot* imagery with clients, I strongly recommend individual study and practice – not only to aid understanding, but also to allow one to witness firsthand the transformative power of the *Tarot*.

Continued study and practice with the *Tarot* naturally cultivate intuition which, whether consciously acknowledged or not, remains an essential tool in therapeutic work.

❦ 7 ❦
CASES

I shall now provide several cases in which I utilised *Tarot* in my Life Coaching and Hypnotherapy practice, as well as during my time working in Co-Occurring Substance Abuse Counselling. Though this was not undertaken in the role of a psychologist, I believe the cases contained herein provide meaningful insights into the implementation of *Tarot* within psychotherapy and professional medical-psychological services.

I once had a client who was undergoing a very turbulent life change. After an episode of binge drinking, she had been involved in a car accident. At the time, she was living out of her vehicle, and the accident destroyed all her personal belongings. She was left with absolutely nothing and had to start again "at square one."

The cards I drew for her were the *Knight of Swords*, *The Tower of Destruction*, and *Strength*. When I invited her to free-associate, she linked the *Knight* with how she "was before," when she "charged toward her destiny." *The Tower* she associated with the recent events, and *Strength* with who she wished to become. The natural sequence of past, present, and future is notable here.

She then began to cry – likely due to the surfacing of repressed emotion – and I shifted from direct hypnotic work to ego-strengthening. That night, she dreamt of a ferocious lion approaching her. As it came nearer, she closed its mouth and rode away upon it. Thus, the lion of the *Tarot* card appeared in her dream. I interpreted this dream holistically as an impetus for her to emerge from the experience stronger and to make use of the tools available to her.

She subsequently utilised her forced relocation to expand her employment opportunities and is now not only sober but also happily working in the vacation industry, in a position that provides comfortable accommodation and meals.

I was conducting Life Coaching with a young girl who was experiencing a turbulent relationship with her mother. The mother was excessively strict and had contributed to the development of the girl's harsh superego. I presented the *Queen of Swords* to her and asked what she thought was happening in the image.

She described an omnipotent, powerful, and terrifying queen who sought the death of her princess daughter and her royal husband. When I asked whether the card reminded her of anyone, she immediately replied, "My mum." Unfortunately, I was unable to continue working with her further, as I lost contact with the father following that session.

My hypnotherapeutic clients often provide very rich material. I once worked with a client in her late thirties who had been married to an unfulfilling man since the age of eighteen. The relationship reached its breaking point during her first and only pregnancy when, during the delivery of her son, her husband was unable to be present in the delivery room as he was occupied in the lobby playing *World of Warcraft*.

Slowly but surely, as their relationship deteriorated emotionally, so too did the home and the world around her. She then asked that I use the *Tarot* as a tool for self-direction and clarity regarding her current situation. *The Tower of Babel* emerged. She identified the two falling figures as herself and her husband, and the crumbling tower as the home they had built together.

After some therapeutic work surrounding this theme, she took a hiatus from hypnotherapy to "rebuild what was lost." A few months later, I was contacted by the same client who had not only broken away from the relationship but had also moved into a new home, lost weight, joined a gym, and begun to prioritise self-growth, independence, and femininity.

When I drew a card to discern where she was emotionally at this time, *The Star* emerged. As of the writing of this book, I continue to work with this client. Following several *Tarot* hypnotherapy sessions, she has become markedly more confident, self-assertive, and self-reliant. She is now open to meeting other men and approaches relationships from a place of self-value rather than reaction or dependence. In time, she suggested meeting once every two weeks, and she remains in a far more elevated state of mind than before.

I once had a client who struggled with stress and anxiety – the former inciting the latter. After some exploration, she identified with the figure of the *Queen of Cups*. She described her stress and anxiety as oceanic waves that pulled her in until they overwhelmed her. In the image, one notices that the queen's dress merges with the water itself.

During hypnotherapy, I asked the client what it was

that the Queen held inside her cup. "Resentment," she replied. When I asked, "Resentment of what?" she answered, "Of having people depend on her."

I then guided the client to assume the form of the Queen and to envision the resentment as water within the cup. I had her pour that resentment out into the sea and feel the lightness of the cup in her hand. Upon emerging from trance, she shared that, since childhood, she had been responsible for raising her younger siblings, being the eldest. This sense of pressure had carried into both her marriage and motherhood. She did not feel she could be vulnerable with anyone, as she always had to be present when others needed her. She had no room to experience her own emotions because she had to be the container for everyone else's.

One or two sessions later, the client reported feeling much better. She gradually individuated from therapy – first attending once every two weeks, then every three, and finally once a month. The last time I spoke with her was a year ago; she informed me that she is now in much better health and enjoys a satisfying, adventurous, and vivacious relationship with her husband, her children, and herself. This case occurred at the beginning of my Life Coaching career, and I continue to regard it as one of the most memorable.

I shall now share my personal experience with the *Tarot*. From a very early age, I was always drawn to reading and writing, and I naturally gravitated towards the subjects in which I now invest most of my time studying. By no later than the age of five, I had begun reading books on psychology, mythology, and the occult. I owe much of this early exposure to the influence of my two older sisters, as well as to the guidance of my mother and grandmother, who were and are deeply familiar with these subjects.

My eldest sister was studying massage therapy at the time and incorporated spirituality into her practice. Her college-level book collection on these topics became, in essence, my personal library. My mother, to whom I have dedicated this book, contributed enormously to my love of study. When I was a child, she would take me to the library and read me poetry, Shakespeare, and the legends of King Arthur. I knew every fable of Andersen and Grimm, and soon became fascinated by folklore and urban legend.

When I would visit my sister, she would have incense sticks and crystals about her house, and I would either inquire about the purpose of these crystals or find out for myself by reading her books. One of the books, I noticed, was different from the others in that it was accompanied by what appeared to be a toy of some sort. Upon closer examination, I saw that this toy was a deck of playing cards, beautifully illustrated with a blue cover and adorned with golden seven-rayed stars.

As I explored these cards further, I noticed that there were vibrant and distinct images painted upon them, each with differing names. I distinctly remember picking up *The Devil* and wondering why it bore such similarity to *The Lovers*, and why some cards had names while others did not. I pondered the meaning of the nameless cards and questioned, with the curiosity of a child, why a man lay upon the ground bleeding with ten swords in his back before the rising sun.

The book was called *Tarot*, and I explored the meanings of the cards with the book as my key. Since my discovery of the *Tarot* at five years old, my interest in it has developed from research to practice. It was my own use of the *Tarot* that facilitated the writing of a spontaneous story hitherto unpublished. I wrote this story by exploring within my imagination the connections between the different images of the *Tarot* and a rather disheartening love experience I was seeking to understand, process, and release. The images allowed for the symbolic expression of certain feelings and situations that had arisen, and the act of writing the book itself became the "working through" process.

8

CONCLUSION

I use the words "analyst", "therapist", "practitioner", and "hypnotherapist" throughout this book, often interchangeably. This does not suggest that all of these titles are equal or synonymous, but rather that the techniques described within these pages can be used by all of the aforementioned professionals and adapted to each of their specific roles.

Although the insights in this book were developed during my final year of undergraduate study and my year of hypnotherapy training, I do not believe this diminishes the value or practical utility of the concepts presented herein. The need to know oneself pervades Life Coaching, Hypnotherapy, Medical Counselling, and Psychotherapy. This need for self-discovery forms the central premise of this book. As the field of Tarot Psychology expands, I expect many similar ideas as those expounded herein to emerge.

It is the duty of the Life Coach, Hypnotherapist, Counsellor, and Therapist to assist in the client's journey towards self-discovery and self-acceptance, thereby helping them to live a more satisfied and confident life.

In Eden, man knew himself. Adam and Eve did not exist in blissful ignorance; rather, they existed in ignorance of evil. Yet to know evil, one must engage in evil. Thus, the words of God and the words of the Serpent take on deeper meaning.

God had spoken to Eve, saying, "Of every tree of the garden thou mayest freely eat: but of the tree of the knowledge of good and evil, thou shalt not eat of it; for in the day that thou eatest thereof thou shalt surely die." The Serpent, however, said to Eve, "Yea, hath God said, Ye shall not eat of every tree of the garden? Ye shall not surely die: for God doth know that in the day ye eat thereof, then your eyes shall be opened, and ye shall be as gods, knowing good and evil."

Life and death to God, and life and death to the Serpent, thus mean the opposite. For to God, what is the path of elevation is, to the Serpent, the path of descent, and vice versa. The author of *Meditations on the Tarot* explains that, because of this, Eve heard not one but two voices in that moment: both the voice of the Serpent and her own inner voice urging her towards illumination.

The Serpent, as a symbol of the Father of Lies, offered a false interpretation of knowledge that ultimately led to a fall from grace, a loss of personal security and awareness. As a practitioner, one must never guide clients towards self-knowledge as if it were a conquest.

Self-discovery is not the building of a tower but the carrying of a cross. As individuals, we must therefore ascend to self-discovery by way of Calvary and not the Tower of Babel. The former provides meaning to suffering, whereas the latter brings suffering to meaning.

We must, then, know ourselves and heed the warning of the Saviour on the Cross:

"Forgive them Father, for they *know not* what they do."

BIBLIOGRAPHY

Abraham, K. (1927). Contributions to the theory of the anal character (1921). In *Selected papers on psycho-analysis* (pp. 371–392). Hogarth Press. (Original work published 1921)

Adair, D. (2019, September 12). 9/11 and the lightning struck Tower. *Just the Tarot*. https://just-the-tarot.com/2019/09/12/9-11-and-the-lightning-struck-tower/

Akhtar, S., Kramer, S., & Parens, H. (Eds.). (1995). *The birth of hatred: Developmental, clinical, and technical aspects of intense aggression*. Northvale, NJ: Jason Aronson.

Akhtar, S. (2009a). Jocasta complex. In *Comprehensive dictionary of psychoanalysis*. Karnac.

Akhtar, S. (2009b). Medea complex. In *Comprehensive dictionary of psychoanalysis*. Karnac.

Akhtar, S. (2009c). Electra complex. In *Comprehensive dictionary of psychoanalysis*. Karnac.

Anastasopoulos, D., Soumaki, E., & Anagnostopoulos, D. (2010). Adolescence and mythology. *Journal of Child Psychotherapy, 36*(2), 119–132. https://doi.org/10.1080/0075417x.2010.495023

Anonymous. (1985). *Meditations on the Tarot: A journey into Christian Hermeticism* (R. A. Powell, Trans.; H. U. von Balthasar, Afterword). Amity House. (Original French work published 1980)

Asprem, E. (2017). Explaining the esoteric imagination: Towards a theory of kataphatic practice. *Aries, 17*(1), 17–50. https://doi.org/10.1163/15700593-01701002

Auger, E. E. (2004). *Tarot and other meditation decks: History, theory, aesthetics, typology*. McFarland.

Bachelard, G. (1948). *La terre et les rêveries de la volonté*. Librairie José Corti.

Barker, S. (2021). Andromeda unchained: Women and erotic mythology in Renaissance art, 1500–1650. In M. Falomir & A. Vergara (Eds.), *Mythological passions: Titian, Veronese, Allori, Rubens, Ribera, Poussin, Van Dyck, Velázquez* (pp. 57–81). Museo Nacional del Prado.

Barraca Mairal, J. (2015). The "Fortunata syndrome": A form of emotional dependency. *Papeles del Psicólogo, 36*(2), 145–152.

Berenbaum, S. A., & Beltz, A. M. (2011). Sexual differentiation of human behavior: Effects of prenatal and pubertal organizational hormones. *Frontiers in Neuroendocrinology, 32*(2), 183–200. https://doi.org/10.1016/j.yfrne.2010.10.002

Berger, A. A. (2005). *Media analysis techniques* (3rd ed.). Sage.

Breuer, J., & Freud, S. (1893/1955). On the psychical mechanism of hysterical phenomena: Preliminary communication. In J. Strachey (Ed. & Trans.), *The standard edition of the complete psychological works of Sigmund Freud* (Vol. 2, pp. 1–17). London: Hogarth Press.

Bruner, J. (1990). *Acts of meaning*. Harvard University Press.

Bruner, J. (1991). Self-making and world-making. *The Journal of Aesthetic Education, 25*(1), 67–78. https://doi.org/10.2307/3333092

Builders of the Adytum. (2022, March). B.O.T.A. centennial article. https://www.bota.org/images/news_events/Zenith_March_2022_Centennial_article-FINAL.pdf

Burr, J. (2016, August 12). *Spiritual tarot: Hypnotic applications for the archetypes of tarot* [Video; recorded July 30, 2016]. American Hypnosis Association.

Case, P. F. (1916). The secret doctrine of the Tarot. *The Word, 23*(4).

Case, P. F. (2006). *The Tarot: A key to the wisdom of the ages*. National Geographic Books.

Cave, T. (1988). *Recognitions: A study in poetics*. Clarendon Press.

Cheek, D. B. (1992a, Summer). Fetal perception and memory. *Institute for Research in Metapsychology Newsletter*. Applied Metapsychology International. https://appliedmetapsychology.org/research-publications/case-studies/fetal-perception-and-memory/

Cheek, D. B. (1992b). Are telepathy, clairvoyance, and "hearing" possible in utero? Suggestive evidence as revealed during hypnotic age-regression studies of prenatal memory. *Pre- and Peri-natal Psychology Journal, 7*(2), 125–137.

Chevalier, J., & Gheerbrant, A. (1996). *The Penguin dictionary of symbols* (J. Buchanan-Brown, Trans.). Penguin.

Cohen, S., & Halberg, A. (Writers & Directors). (2024). *Tarot* [Film]. Screen Gems; Alloy Entertainment.

Cooper, J. C. (1987). *An illustrated encyclopaedia of traditional symbols*. Thames & Hudson.

Dahl, E. K. (1989). Daughters and mothers: Oedipal aspects of the witch-mother. *The Psychoanalytic Study of the Child, 44*, 267–280.

de Justin, B. (2024, December 20). A psychoanalytic interpretation of devotion to the sacred heart. *Bryan de Justin*. https://www.bryandejustincoaching.com/post/a-psychoanalytic-interpretation-of-devotion-to-the-sacred-heart-catholic-psychoanalysis

De Vleminck, J. (2013a). "In the beginning was the Deed": On Oedipus and Cain. In V. Zajko & E. O'Gorman (Eds.), *Classical myth and psychoanalysis: Ancient and modern stories of the self* (pp. 265–282). Oxford University Press.

De Vleminck, J. (2013b). Szondi's mythological unconscious. In V. M.

Zelizer (Ed.), *Classical myth and psychoanalysis: Ancient and modern stories of the self* (pp. 258–277). Oxford University Press.

Douay–Rheims Bible. (2003). *The Holy Bible: Douay–Rheims Version*. Baronius Press. (Original work published 1899)

Dundes, A. (1969). Folklore as a mirror of culture. *Elementary English, 46*(4), 471–482.

Dundes, A. (1979). The number three in American culture. In *Analytic essays in folklore* (pp. 206–225). De Gruyter Mouton. https://doi.org/10.1515/9783110903768-022

Dundes, A. (1980). *Interpreting folklore*. Indiana University Press.

Dundes, A. (2009). *Bloody Mary in the mirror: Essays in psychoanalytic folkloristics*. University Press of Mississippi.

Eber, M. (1981). Don Juanism: A disorder of the self. *Bulletin of the Menninger Clinic, 45*(4), 307–316.

Ellis, H. (1906). *Studies in the psychology of sex: Vol. 5. Erotic symbolism; The mechanism of detumescence; The psychic state in pregnancy*. F. A. Davis.

Fortune, D. (1930). *Psychic self-defence: A study in occult pathology and criminality*. Rider & Co.

Fortune, D. (2010). *The demon lover* (D. L. Paxson, Foreword). Weiser Books. (Original work published 1927).

Freud, A. (1965). *Normality and pathology in childhood: Assessments of development*. International Universities Press.

Freud, S. (1898/1955). Sexuality in the aetiology of the neuroses. In J. Strachey (Ed. & Trans.), *The Standard Edition of the Complete Psychological Works of Sigmund Freud* (Vol. 3, pp. 259–285). London: Hogarth Press.

Freud, S. (1908/1959). Character and anal erotism. In J. Strachey (Ed. & Trans.), *The standard edition of the complete psychological works of Sigmund Freud* (Vol. 9, pp. 167–176). Hogarth Press. (Original work published 1908)

Freud, S. (1909/1955). Analysis of a phobia in a five-year-old boy. In J. Strachey (Ed. & Trans.), *The standard edition of the complete psychological works of Sigmund Freud* (Vol. 10, pp. 3–149). Hogarth Press. (Original work published 1909)

Freud, S. (1910). The origin and development of psychoanalysis. *American Journal of Psychology, 21*, 181–218.

Freud, S. (1911/1958). Psycho-analytic notes upon an autobiographical account of a case of paranoia (Dementia paranoides). In J. Strachey (Ed. & Trans.), *The standard edition of the complete psychological works of Sigmund Freud* (Vol. 12, pp. 1–82). Hogarth Press. (Original work published 1911)

Freud, S. (1912/1957). On the universal tendency to debasement in the sphere of love (Contributions to the psychology of love II). In J. Strachey (Ed. & Trans.), *The standard edition of the complete psychological works of Sigmund Freud* (Vol. 11, pp. 177–190). Hogarth Press. (Original work published 1912)

Freud, S. (1913/1955). *Totem and taboo: Some points of agreement between the mental lives of savages and neurotics.* In J. Strachey (Ed. & Trans.), *The standard edition of the complete psychological works of Sigmund Freud* (Vol. 13, pp. 1–161). London: Hogarth Press. (Original work published 1913).

Freud, S. (1914/1957). On narcissism: An introduction. In J. Strachey (Ed. & Trans.), *The standard edition of the complete psychological works of Sigmund Freud* (Vol. 14, pp. 67–102). Hogarth Press. (Original work published 1914)

Freud, S. (1915/1957). Instincts and their vicissitudes. In J. Strachey (Ed. & Trans.), *The standard edition of the complete psychological works of Sigmund Freud* (Vol. 14, pp. 109–140). Hogarth Press. (Original work published 1915)

Freud, S. (1920/1955). Beyond the pleasure principle. In J. Strachey (Ed. & Trans.), *The standard edition of the complete psychological works of Sigmund Freud* (Vol. 18, pp. 1–64). Hogarth Press. (Original work published 1920)

Freud, S. (1922/1955). Dreams and telepathy (J. Strachey, Ed. & Trans.). In *The standard edition of the complete psychological works of Sigmund Freud* (Vol. 18, pp. 195–220). Hogarth Press. (Original work published 1922)

Freud, S. (1922/1955). Medusa's head. In J. Strachey (Ed. & Trans.), *The standard edition of the complete psychological works of Sigmund Freud* (Vol. 18, pp. 273–274). London: The Hogarth Press. (Original work written 1922; first published 1940)

Freud, S. (1923/1961). The ego and the id. In J. Strachey (Ed. & Trans.), *The standard edition of the complete psychological works of Sigmund Freud* (Vol. 19, pp. 12–66). Hogarth Press. (Original work published 1923)

Freud, S. (1924/1961). The dissolution of the Oedipus complex. In J. Strachey (Ed. & Trans.), *The standard edition of the complete psychological works of Sigmund Freud* (Vol. 19, pp. 171–180). Hogarth Press. (Original work published 1924)

Freud, S. (1930/1961). Civilization and its discontents (J. Strachey, Trans.). In J. Strachey (Ed.), *The standard edition of the complete psychological works of Sigmund Freud* (Vol. 21, pp. 64–145). Hogarth Press. (Original work published 1930)

Freud, S. (1931/1961). Libidinal types. In J. Strachey (Ed. & Trans.), *The standard edition of the complete psychological works of Sigmund Freud* (Vol. 21, pp. 215–220). Hogarth Press. (Original work published 1931)

Freud, S. (1933/1964). New introductory lectures on psycho-analysis (Lecture 31, "The dissection of the psychical personality"). In J. Strachey (Ed. & Trans.), *The standard edition of the complete psychological works of Sigmund Freud*(Vol. 22, pp. 57–144). Hogarth Press. (Original work published 1933)

Freud, S. (1935). New introductory lectures on psycho-analysis. *Archives of Neurology and Psychiatry, 33*(5), 1135. https://doi.org/10.1001/archneurpsyc.1935.02250170221019

Freud, S. (1939). *Moses and monotheism* (K. Jones, Trans.). The Hogarth Press & The Institute of Psycho-Analysis.

Freud, S. (1953). Three essays on the theory of sexuality (J. Strachey, Ed. & Trans.). In J. Strachey (Ed. & Trans.), *The standard edition of the complete psychological works of Sigmund Freud* (Vol. 7, pp. 123–246). Hogarth Press. (Original work published 1905)

Freud, S. (2010). *The interpretation of dreams: The complete and definitive text* (J. Strachey, Trans.). Basic Books. (Original work published 1900)

Friedman, P. (Ed. & Trans.). (1967). *On suicide: With particular reference to suicide among young students*. International Universities Press.

Fromm, E. (1990). *Man for himself: An inquiry into the psychology of ethics*. Henry Holt and Company. (Original work published 1947)

Gigerenzer, G. (2014). Cassandra's regret: The psychology of not wanting to know. *Psychological Review, 121*(4), 505–517.

Gierczyk, M., & Dobosz, D. (2022). Functioning of Polish women in binational relationships—An outline of the issue against the background of migration in the interpreted paradigm. *Humans, 2*(2), 50–63. https://doi.org/10.3390/humans2020004

Gordillo, F., Molina, D., & Prieto, J. (2020). Megalomania, grandeur delusions and the "Messiah complex": A case report. *International Journal of Psychiatry Research, 3*(5), 1–4.

Hartmann. (1895). [Note on double monstrosity after maternal impression]. *Münchener Medizinische Wochenschrift,* (9). As cited in Ellis (1906, p. 122).

Havlíček, J., Husárová, B., Řezáčová, V., & Klapilová, K. (2011). Correlates of extra-dyadic sex in Czech heterosexual couples: Does sexual behavior of parents matter? *Archives of Sexual Behavior, 40*(6), 1153–1163. https://doi.org/10.1007/s10508-011-9869-3

Hilgard, J. R. (1953). Anniversary reactions in parents precipitated by children. *Psychiatry, 16*(1), 73–80. https://doi.org/10.1080/00332747.1953.11022910

Hooke, S. H. (1939). Cain and Abel. *Folklore, 50*(1), 58–65. https://doi.org/10.1080/0015587X.1939.9718149

Hughes, R. (1979). Szondi's theory of the Cain complex. *American Imago, 36*(3), 260–274.

Hughes, R. A. (2007). Schicksalsanalyse and religion studies. *The Journal of Religion, 87*(1), 59–78. https://doi.org/10.1086/512196

Ihnat, K. (2016). Mary as Bride in the Old Hispanic Office: Liturgical and Theological Trends. *Mediaeval Studies, 78,* 65–106.

Jacobson, E. (1950). Development of the Wish for a Child in Boys. *The*

Psychoanalytic Study of the Child, 5(1), 139–152. https://doi.org/10.1080/00797308.1950.11822889

Jay, J. (2014). *The tragic in Mark: A literary-historical interpretation*. Mohr Siebeck.

Jenkyns, J. (1895, March 2). [Letter on maternal impressions and polydactyly (supernumerary digit)]. *British Medical Journal, 1*(1783). As cited in Ellis (1906, p. 122).

Jensen, K. F. (2005). The early Waite–Smith tarot editions. *The Playing-Card: Journal of the International Playing-Card Society*. https://www.arnellart.com/manteia/waite-smith/tpc-article.pdf

Jones, E. (1953). *The life and work of Sigmund Freud: Vol. 1. The formative years and the great discoveries, 1856–1900*. Basic Books.

Jung, C. G. (1938). *Psychology and religion*. Yale University Press. (Also available as: Jung, C. G. (1969). *Psychology and religion: West and East ... Collected Works* (Vol. 11). Princeton University Press.)

Jung, C. G. (1963). *Memories, dreams, reflections*. Collins.

Jung, C. G. (1967). *Symbols of transformation* (R. F. C. Hull, Trans.; H. Read, M. Fordham, & G. Adler, Eds.; 2nd ed.). *The Collected Works of C. G. Jung* (Vol. 5). Princeton University Press. (Original work published 1912)

Jung, C. G. (1969). *The archetypes and the collective unconscious* (R. F. C. Hull, Trans.; H. Read, M. Fordham, & G. Adler, Eds.; 2nd ed.). The Collected Works of C. G. Jung (Vol. 9, Pt. 1). Princeton University Press. (Original essays published 1934–1954).

Jung, C. G. (1971). *Psychological types* (R. F. C. Hull, Trans.; H. Read, M. Fordham, & G. Adler, Eds.). The Collected Works of C. G. Jung (Vol. 6). Princeton University Press. (Original work published 1921).

Jung, C. G. (1972). The structure of the psyche (R. F. C. Hull, Trans.). In H. Read, M. Fordham, & G. Adler (Eds.), *The Collected Works of C. G. Jung* (2nd ed., Vol. 8, pp. 139–158). Princeton University Press. (Original work published 1927; revised 1931).

Jung, C. G. (1997). *Visions: Notes of the seminar given in 1930–1934* (Vol. 2, C. Douglas, Ed.). Princeton University Press.

Kahn, C. (1981). *Man's estate: Masculine identity in Shakespeare* (esp. "Self and Eros in 'Venus and Adonis,'" pp. 21–46). University of California Press.

Keirsey, D., & Bates, M. (1984). *Please understand me: Character and temperament types* (5th ed.). Prometheus Nemesis. (First ed. 1978)

Kitahara, M. (1976) *A cross-cultural test of the Freudian theory of circumcision. International Journal of Psychoanalytic Psychotherapy, 5,* 535–546

Klein, M. (2002). *Love, guilt and reparation: And other works 1921–1945*. Simon & Schuster.

Knapen, J. E. P., Blaker, N. M., & Van Vugt, M. (2018). The Napoleon complex: When shorter men take more. *Psychological Science, 29*(7), 1134–1144. https://doi.org/10.1177/0956797618772822

Kretschmer, E. (1925). *Physique and character: An investigation of the nature of constitution and of the theory of temperament*. Kegan Paul, Trench, Trubner. (Original work published 1921 as *Körperbau und Charakter*)

Laplanche, J. (1999). *Essays on otherness*. Routledge.

Lowenfeld, M. F. (1950). The nature and use of the Lowenfeld World Technique in work with children and adults. *The Journal of Psychology, 30*(2), 325–331.

Maccoby, M. (2002). Toward a science of social character. *International Forum of Psychoanalysis, 11*(1), 33–44. (Earlier version: *Fromm Forum 5*, 2001)

Mackay, A. (1891, December 19). [Case note on maternal impression: Hare thrown at pregnant woman; infant with hare-like cheek patch]. *The Lancet*. As cited in Ellis (1906, p. 122).

Mairal, G. (2015). The Fortunata syndrome (complex): Women in love with married men. [Publication information not specified].

Mathers, S. L. M., & Felkin, H. (n.d.). *Book T: The tarot—Comprising manuscripts N, O, P, Q, R, and an unlettered Theoricus Adeptus Minor instruction* [Unpublished manuscript]. (Original work circulated in the 1890s)

McAdams, D. P. (1993). *The stories we live by: Personal myths and the making of the self*. William Morrow.

McAdams, D. P. (2001). The psychology of life stories. *Review of General Psychology, 5*(2), 100–122. https://doi.org/10.1037/1089-2680.5.2.100

Mendel, A. O. (1949). Symbolism in handwriting. *The Psychoanalytic Review, 36*(3), 255–259.

Meyer, M. (1989). *The Alexander complex*. Times Books.

Moore, K. L., Persaud, T. V. N., & Torchia, M. G. (2020). *The developing human: Clinically oriented embryology* (11th ed.). Elsevier.

National Park Service. (2025, July 29). Park statistics – Statue of Liberty National Monument. https://www.nps.gov/stli/learn/management/park-statistics.htm

Neumann, E. (2014). *The origins and history of consciousness* (R. F. C. Hull, Trans.). Princeton University Press. (Original work published 1954)

Nichols, S. (1980). *Jung and tarot: An archetypal journey*. Weiser Books.

Ouspensky, P. D. (1913). *The symbolism of the tarot: Philosophy of occultism in pictures and numbers; Pen-pictures of the twenty-two tarot cards* (A. L. Pogossky, Trans.). Trood Printing and Publishing Company.

Pattnaik, P., & Al Khalili, Y. (2025). Moro reflex. In *StatPearls*. StatPearls Publishing. https://www.ncbi.nlm.nih.gov/books/NBK542173/

Polhemus, R. M. (2005). *Lot's daughters: Sex, redemption, and women's quest for authority*. Stanford University Press.

Pollock, G. H. (1970). Anniversary reactions, trauma and mourning. *The Psychoanalytic Quarterly, 39*(3), 347–371.

Porter, E. H. (1976). On the development of Relationship Awareness

Theory: A personal note. *Group & Organization Studies, 1*(3), 302–309. https://doi.org/10.1177/105960117600100305

Rank, O. (1914). *The myth of the birth of the hero: A psychological interpretation of mythology* (F. Robbins & S. E. Jelliffe, Trans.). The Journal of Nervous and Mental Disease Publishing Company. (Original work published 1909).

Rank, O. (1993). *The trauma of birth* (E. J. Lieberman, Intro.). Dover Publications. (Original work published 1924; English trans. 1929)

Rancour-Laferriere, D. (2018). *Imagining Mary: A psychoanalytic perspective on devotion to the Virgin Mother of God.* Routledge.

Rebhorn, W. A. (1978). Mother Venus: Temptation in Shakespeare's *Venus and Adonis*. *Shakespeare Studies, 11,* 1–19.

Reichbart, R. H. (1983). *Heart symbolism: An investigation into psychoanalytic symbolism as applied to the heart* (Doctoral dissertation, City University of New York). ProQuest Dissertations & Theses Global.

Rice, R. (2022). *Video games in psychotherapy.* Taylor & Francis.

Ricoeur, P. (1974). Existence and hermeneutics (K. McLaughlin, Trans.). In D. Ihde (Ed.), *The conflict of interpretations: Essays in hermeneutics* (pp. 3–24). Northwestern University Press. (Original work published 1969)

Rizq, R. (2022). Epistemologies of the particular: Psychoanalysis and Tessa Hadley's "An Abduction." *Psychodynamic Practice, 28*(1), 8–24. https://doi.org/10.1080/14753634.2021.2003718

Rosengarten, A. (2000). *Tarot and psychology: Spectrums of possibility.* Paragon House.

Ross, J. M. (1982). Oedipus revisited: Laius and the "Laius complex." *Psychoanalytic Study of the Child, 37,* 169–200.

Sisk, C. L., & Zehr, J. L. (2005). Pubertal hormones organize the adolescent brain and behavior. *Frontiers in Neuroendocrinology, 26*(3–4), 163–174.

Spotnitz, H. (1962). The need for insulation in the schizophrenic personality. *The Psychoanalytic Review, 49*(3), 3–25.

Spotnitz, H. (1976). The need for insulation. In *Psychotherapy of preoedipal conditions: Schizophrenia and severe character disorders* (pp. 117–136). Jason Aronson.

Stahl, F. A. (1896, April). [Case of anencephaly following maternal fright]. *American Journal of Obstetrics and Diseases of Women and Children.* As cited in Ellis (1906, p. 122).

Swaab, D. F. (2004). Sexual differentiation of the human brain: Relevance for gender identity, transsexualism and sexual orientation. *Gynecological Endocrinology, 19*(6), 301–312. https://doi.org/10.1080/09513590400018248

Szondi, L. (1964). Thanatos and Cain (M. W. Webb, Trans.). *American Imago, 21*(3–4), 52–63.

Szondi, L. (1969). *Kain: Gestalten des Bösen*. [See also Szondi, 1973, *Moses: Antwort auf Kain.*]

Szondi, L. (2011). *Ego analysis: The foundation for the union of depth psychologies* (A. C. Johnston, Trans.). Szondi Forum. https://www.szondiforum.org/I.%20Ego%20Analysis.pdf (Original work published 1956)

Teresa of Ávila. (2008). The book of her life (K. Kavanaugh & O. Rodriguez, Trans.). In *The collected works of St. Teresa of Ávila* (Vol. 1, 2nd ed., pp. 1–326). ICS Publications. (Original work published 1565)

Todd, J., & Dewhurst, K. (1955). The Othello syndrome: A study in the psychopathology of sexual jealousy. *Journal of Nervous and Mental Disease, 122*(4), 367–374.

Waite, A. E. (1959). *The pictorial key to the tarot: Being fragments of a secret tradition under the veil of divination*. University Books.

Wang, R., & Wang, Y. (2008). *Tarot psychology*. Marcus Aurelius Press.

Yılmaz, T. U., Taş, H. İ., Uçar, E., Cerit, C., Çelebi, A., Güler, S. A., & Utkan, Z. (2019). Relationship between functional constipation and anal-retentive behavior features. *Turkish Journal of Surgery, 35*(3), 165–170. https://doi.org/10.5578/turkjsurg.4035

www.ingramcontent.com/pod-product-compliance
Lightning Source LLC
Chambersburg PA
CBHW070935180426
43192CB00039B/2203